A

Voice

Which

Uses

No

Words

Lucas Handwerker

Persistent Publishing

ISBN: 9780578422176

Noblet and *Dodal Tarot de Marseille* images courtesy of

letarot.com and the JC Flornoy Estate

Contents

1. The Rocks That Grow...7

2. A Word.. 9

3. A Psychic and a Shaman Walk Into a Bar............. 17

4. The Anatomy of An Intuitive Reading................... 47

5. The Trail is Beautiful, Be Still............................ 75

6. Zap, Apprehension, Career, Hell........................... 103

7. The Rocks That Grow Again................................. 133

8. Special Thanks... 136

9. Bibliography...137

"What if you slept
And what if
In your sleep
You dreamed
And what if
In your dream
You went to heaven
And there plucked a strange and
beautiful flower
And what if
When you awoke
You had that flower in your hand.
Ah, what then?"

-Samuel Taylor Coleridge

1

The Rocks That Grow

Have you seen the rocks that grow? They sit by the black water on the full moon. It's an optical illusion. I dreamt there was a storm out over the waves. It felt primordial like it wanted to eat me. I wanted to get a better look so I walked into the ocean with my boots on. Seawater rushed between my toes and soles.

I walked down the sand and saw an older man with salt and pepper hair dressed as a cowboy. He was holding a prayer candle. The glow of the candle lit up the cracks in his face, it looked like the Grand

Canyon. He was walking in circles. It seemed like he was looking for something.

I walked up to him and asked what he was looking for. He looked up at me and held my gaze for what felt like a long time. He looked confused. Then he said, "I'm not looking for anything."

At that moment I realized that I was looking for something. I was looking for my jacket. I looked down and realized I was now holding my jacket.

The cowboy looked at me like my face was on backward. He said something to me in a voice which sounded like sand and salt. But just before I could make out what he was saying, the phone rang and woke me up.

2

A Word

Leading up to my thirteenth birthday I wondered how my superpowers would develop. Maybe a near-death experience would bring them out. When I turned thirteen and I wasn't able to fly I felt a little disappointed. I quickly realized a lot of people don't get their powers until they're eighteen. Five more years in anticipation lead to another disappointing birthday.

Maybe twenty-one would be the year, I thought, fully aware that this was steadily becoming ridiculous.

When I was small, smaller than I am now, I would walk through crowds in sheer terror. Everything was warped and intensified. Someone looking at me from across the room felt as if they were up against my nose. I felt. I felt deeply what everyone around me was feeling. Any apprehension, anger, uneasiness, fear, or depression was absorbed by my little arms and hands. I had a firm grip on feelings too big for my little pink fingers.

I felt all those grown-up feelings, swirling around me like a wind made up of woe and tumultuousness. It whipped around and smacked me right in my baby teeth. Every muscle in my body would tense and reject.

I was sensitive. I could only fix my eyes to the ground and hide behind my parents. I felt all these grown-up feelings as my own. I didn't know they weren't my feelings to carry.

I found myself hiding in my room most days, afraid of the outside world and all its swirling energies. It was years before I realized that being sensitive was not some terrible curse but a responsibility. A responsibility, that with some practice, and control could become like a real life super power.

With control and direction, this sensitivity could become something closer to intuition. I could feel what people were feeling. All I had to do was remember that what I was feeling didn't belong to me. If I could do that I would have a sense of anyone I walked past. If I spent more time with someone, I could feel where they were emotionally; how they were feeling about themselves, their lives, their relationships.

I only felt these things vaguely, in the way, you sense something in a dream. You know without any immediate evidence in a dream. You just know. That's how I was able to feel what someone in front of me was feeling. But I had no language to communicate it with. I searched for a way to frame my feelings in a beautiful and productive way.

In giving an intuitive reading I was able to turn my feelings into visual stories, metaphors, and iconographic poems. With the format of an intuitive reading, my intuition was given a language to speak. My intuition was supplied a translator and an advocate. My intuition was given a stage to affect individuals and crowds. I was no longer walking looking at the ground. I was walking looking at the sky. I had found my superpower.

Wut?

But what the hell is intuition? It's more a feeling than a thing. A memory than a definition. Intuition has directed so much of my life. From the decisions I've made, to the work I do now as an intuitive reader. But what the hell is it? I'm not so sure.

The early use of the word comes from the Latin root *intueri* or "to consider." It generally had an association with spiritual consideration, meditation, and contemplation. Usually contemplation on a spiritual ideal. So at its very root, intuition is about connecting to something beyond yourself– whether you call it God the universe, spirit, some esoteric force, or simply the world of symbol.

Beyond contemplation, intuition is a means of connection to another human being. A way to direct their path. I'm still not entirely sure. That's part of the value and the beauty of intuition. Intuition is the freedom to not be sure and in that uncertainty, in that yielding, to be clearer, more connected and more directed than any amount of certainty can ever offer.

Intuition has become a compass, map, and spiritual practice. It's a way of living. A way of seeing. Seeing with inner feeling. It's a way of hearing a voice. It's a way of listening to a voice. A voice inside all of us, and yet completely outside. A voice which uses no words.

Another Word

The best way for me to talk about intuition is to show you how I use it. For a long time, I resisted intuition as a true and formal tool. I have since found it my most cherished companion.

My intuition was like a friend I always had but often ignored. I've found only good things through my intuition. I've faced only bad things when I've neglected it. I am stunned whenever I use it.

I still remember my first intuitive reading. It was at a house party in Woodstock, New York. I looked at a woman I was working with, standing in front of a room of people. I felt three ideas enter my mind. Energy, Valentines Day, aneurysm. I hesitantly accepted what my intuition had to offer and did my best to work with it.

"Something happened recently. Maybe something medical? It happened around or on

Valentine's Day. It may have had to do with your romantic life in some way. Ultimately this event had you begin to reconsider how you spend your energy and your time. Does that make sense?"

She looked at me in stunned silence and said: "Yes." I was pleasantly surprised. In my excitement, I asked if she would share more with the group. She told us that on Valentine's Day she had a breast cancer scare, and had to go to the hospital to check everything out. She was ultimately okay, but it made her begin to question how she spent her time and with whom she spent it.

I heard waves of gasps and nervous laughter sweep the room. I was as shocked as the rest of the crowd. I knew from that moment on, there would be no turning back. Intuition was here to stay.

The Very Best Nature

I came to give intuitive readings by leaning into something I've often found troubling; psychic readings. The general format has taken a profound hold on me though. Sitting down with someone and clearing a pathway in their life that's light-filled and hopeful is a beautiful way to spend time.

Intuitive readings have shown me people's best qualities. People laugh, cry, and then begin glowing. I've seen so much tenderness, humanity, and authenticity in everyone I've ever given a reading for. I imagine those qualities lie in waiting within all of us.

What follows is a composite of real readings I've had with real people, as well as real conversations I've had in the past. I've left out certain details, as well as names for the sake of privacy.

3

A Psychic and a Shaman Walk Into a Bar

> *"Knowing depends on
> the time spent looking"*
> -Rumi

I was sitting alone at a bar outside of Woodstock, New York waiting for my sitter to arrive. It was a quiet night and I could hear the crickets outside helping themselves to some more stale beer. I looked at the suds above my drink and saw patterns. Images swirled around. It was like looking at the clouds and seeing animals. My sitter arrived in a black shawl, sat down and ordered a stiff drink.

"Nice to meet you! How're you?" she said through a smile. She sat down hanging her bag off the back of the chair.

"It's good to meet you! I'm well, I like your bracelet," I said in one breath, pointing to her wrist. She was wearing a silver bracelet with turquoise gems.

"Thank you! I got it at a flea market a few years ago" She took it off and handed it to me. I held the cold slim bracelet between my palms and closed my eyes. I felt an immediate warmth wash over me– a sleepy cascading presence over my face. I felt myself melt into the air around me.

In the darkness of my eyelids, I began to see an image. An image in the way you'd see an image in your imagination. There but not there. Vivid, yet translucent. I saw a small kid climbing a chain link fence, moving towards a taller brick wall behind it. Below the child were a dozen or so kids all egging him on, shouting for him to keep climbing. I opened my eyes and told her what I had seen.

"That's really freaky." she responded. "In my old neighborhood growing up, there was a kind of right of passage where everyone had to climb this tall fence. It was next to a large brick wall. And all the kids would stand around cheering them on." I handed her bracelet back.

"How long have you had these gifts?" she asked, putting her bracelet back on, adjusting its tightness.

"Gifts make me think of psychics. I've always felt uncomfortable with psychics. The word itself comes from the Greek psykhe relating to the soul or spirit. So to be a psychic is to be of the soul or spirit." I took a drink of my beer but spilled a little. The liquid on the table looked like the silhouette of a man climbing a tree.

"That's interesting, so why don't you like it then?" she asked, as her drink arrived perfectly placed atop a small square napkin.

"Well, the modern use of the term is widespread and has since been spoiled by less than authentic practitioners and people claiming to have special gifts. My main issue with the term psychic is that it denotes someone with a special ability that others may not have." I took a pause, looking up towards the crown molding on the tin ceilings to gather my thoughts.

She took a long slow drink from her dewy glass gently placing it down just a little closer to me than it had been before. "That sounds like an ego trip and the antithesis to the original meaning," she said pulling off a smear of vodka from her lower lip.

I picked up my napkin and continued. "Exactly. We all have souls. We all have access to these places within ourselves. We all have intuition. I've come to have a great distaste for the idea of intuition as a gift. Intuition is not a gift."

"Well, sorryy." she interrupted with both hands in the air and a sly smile.

"Intuition is closer to a muscle. I guess you could call it a gift we all have." I continued. "Some people are inherently stronger than others. It's like baseball."

"Baseball huh?" she interjected, sipping her drink playfully.

"Anyone can play baseball." I continued. "With a little practice and some work. Some people are more naturally gifted, for sure. Some are more inclined. But anyone can become strong with some practice and some work. It's not even something that requires aligning your chakras or astrally projecting. Although those things can be nice. Intuition is something everyone is already connected to."

"Or disconnected from," she said pointing to the sky.

"I suppose so." I continued, "After a while of being disconnected the connection can feel a bit rusty. Most people feel things every day. Things we can't explain. A sense of knowing. We see patterns in the clouds or the leaves of tea at the bottom of a mug.

"Or the bottom of a glass," she said taking the last sip and putting her empty drink down.

I took another sip from my now flat beer. "Well this idea that things can only be connected by physical means, cause and effect, is a relatively new one. Human beings used to believe in the interconnectedness of all things, regardless of direct cause and effect. That's where this idea of fortune telling came from."

"If everything is connected then the shape of the clouds could determine the health of a child and the patterns in tea leaves could tell who would win an electio--"Just at this moment, a gray-haired man spilled his drink so severely that it reached the other end of the bar. Without reacting at all he began singing *que, sera, sera, whatever will be will be, the future's not ours to see, que sera, sera.* The bartender rushed over with an oversized rag, wiping up the mess.

We regained our attention and carried on. "Because everything is related, one pattern infers another?" she added, immediately unsure.

"Yes! I much prefer intuitive over psychic though. It's truer to the essence of what a reading is. We all have those experiences. An intuitive reader is just someone who's more practiced and has built the muscles. They're also neutral to the one getting the reading."

"That's another thing, it's best not to give yourself readings. You can't be neutral because you know what you want to see, at least unconsciously. So giving yourself a reading doesn't have much use. One of the many values of an intuitive reading is it transcends traditional logic and fixed ways of thinking. A reading shatters pre-set patterns of knowing. It can even shatter others' influence over our seeing. The best reading you can give to yourself is to just remember your dreams at night."

Here, There, and Everywhere

She swirled the stem of her empty glass looking at the remnants of the liquid inside. "I remember once I had a dream I was riding a merry go round in central park with a dog. Now I didn't have a dog at the time, but I could feel his brown fur between my fingers in the dream. The Beatles were playing as the ride went. It was *Here, There, and Everywhere.* You know the song?"

"Two days later I'd completely forgotten my dream. I'm cutting through the park to get to the museum and I see a merry go round. I decide to take a ride. The fourth or fifth time around a little brown dog jumps on the ride. I get a little scared he'll fall off so I pick him up. At that very moment, the same Beatles song plays. *Here, There, and Everywhere.* I am hit instantly with an overwhelming sense of deja vu. This all feels so familiar, you know? Then I remember, I remember the dream I had forgotten. I had experienced it before, but in my dream."

"They say you're everyone in your dreams," I interjected. "That's not too uncommon for a healer to have those kinds of experiences as they develop their powers. The first form of intuitive readings were dreams. Shamans and oracles would have dreams or visions and they'd interpret the images to develop a reading."

"Even as far back as ancient Egypt, they would build *sleep temples* in the name of Imhotep, a holy physician priest. People would come into these *sleep temples* with issues and stay several nights to have their dreams analyzed in order to find a solution."

"Oh, so the sitter became the reader?" she said, kicking her shoes off under the table.

"Every reading is directed by the sitter, it's their experience," I said pushing my chair out to give her stocking feet more room. "That's another distinction between a psychic and an intuitive reader. A psychic reading puts the emphasis on what the reader says and offers. Their word becomes what will be. An intuitive reading is much more centered on the experience and intentions of the sitter. The intuitive reader is just the guide."

"But anyway, these kinds of *sleep temples* which involved chanting, praying, altered states, and dream analysis were also found in ancient Greece as *Asclepieions*. They were healing temples in the name of *Asclepios,* the Greek God of medicine."

She nodded. "So they'd predict the future?" she said, as she removed her shawl and put it on the back of the chair.

"Well sometimes. But the intuitive readings I give aren't about seeing the future. It's about giving people perspective and clarity on any area or issue facing their lives in the past, present, or future."

"To predict the future is to change it. To know the future is to control it. That's not the purpose of a reading. The purpose of a reading is to allow people to know their *relationship* to the future. In doing so we give people more power and understanding over their futures."

"It brings up in them their unconscious concerns, but it also gives them guidance as to how to approach those issues. But to even define a reading in those concrete terms is limiting. A reading is so much to so many different people, and is *never* fixed."

A Living Dream

"In the same way a dream gives us hints as to where to turn, what to do, and what's bugging us, a reading creates a dream and reveals a path."

"A living dream huh?" She leaned back in her chair and put her hands on her head looking up.

"A reading is living in the sense that we are consciously creating it as we experience it. We create it and it creates us."

I continued, "I come to create the dream for them with the question as the frame. The dream is alive and changes with their experience of it. The reading breaths with them."

I paused for a moment considering ordering another drink. "So much about intuition is about paying attention; seeing the meaning. It's about seeing form when others only see the function. Seeing interconnectedness where others see detachment. It requires something of an altered state, as we see with *sleep temples*."

"Do you see those things all the time? Sounds like it could be tiring." she inquired.

"When I started to gain mastery over my intuition I began noticing things in my everyday life. For example, I had this completely bizarre experience recently. I called my mom afterward to make sure I wasn't going crazy. I just had a fight with my girlfriend and left the house to drive to the grocery store. As soon as I stepped outside a perfectly sunny day turned into a sudden rainstorm. I got to an intersection and I was trying to merge into traffic. I looked up and saw two rainbows intersecting. At that moment a bolt of lightning struck through them. I then instinctually turned to my left to see a tall slender man. But his nose was missing. I think he had suffered an injury."

"To this man's right, down the sidewalk, was a little girl with pigtails. She was jumping up and down screaming and pointing. I first thought she was pointing at the man with no nose. But she jumped into his arms as he began to comfort her. She kept pointing in his arms at a large rat running down the sidewalk. It ran past them as her finger continued to follow it. The rat ran into the street and was immediately hit by an oncoming car, rolling over onto its back. I turned to look forward, a little stunned by the sequence of events. I wasn't sure if I had been dreaming or not."

"Are you sure this happened in real life?"

"I'm not totally sure but I'm sure I was waking. Not sleeping"

"It sounds like that event was about the rat, not you. But can you give a reading to gain clarity on a future event?" she asked, trying to make her question sound purely academic.

I nodded silently.

She continued. "I once went to see a *curandero* in Mexico. A shaman down there. He went into a kind of trance, praying and singing, connecting to the heavens and the stars. When he was ready he picked up kernels of maize and tossed them on the table. He looked into the patterns to know what the prognosis was. With each toss, he could deliver more guidance."

She continued. "It seems like you're playing the role of a shaman more than that of a psychic, right?"

"I'd totally agree. A psychic is taking credit for, and accepting the responsibility of, whatever their gifts tell them. A shaman is more a facilitator to help guide people using intuition. A huge part of what a shaman would do, and still does, is give divinatory readings. It's less fortune telling and more spiritual, emotional, or physical diagnosis. What the sitter needs to focus on, or how they should move through an issue or a situation, or a treatment for an ailment. But I don't know I'm a shaman. I'm not equipped to give medical advice. I'm an intuitive reader."

Symbiotic Meaning

She paused for a moment. "You know, I once saw a palm reader in the city. She held my hands and used a crystal to look at the lines on them. She said I would be rich by the time I was twenty-eight. She said I was creative and all that. Said that I was on the right path– already with my soul-mate, even though I was single at the time. But the really funny thing is, a few hours later, I came back with a friend of mine, and she went in while I waited outside. The psychic told my friend the exact same stuff, almost word for word. Actually, hold on a minute. I'll be right back."

She excused herself to order another drink. I took out my notepad and a black pen. I began playing with words that started with the letters in her name.

Below the words, I wrote a few tarot cards that came to mind. It was all followed by some numbers, names, and a handful of other images that floated through. She returned with a fresh drink and placed it on the table, atop a crisp white bar napkin.

"Sorry about that," she said as she took out a pad to take notes with.

"No problem" I instantly responded as I grabbed her first napkin. I drew a large capital letter 'I' on it with my black pen.

"The Hindu sacred book, the *Upanishad*, tells this story of before the creation of the universe. There was one all being entity. A God of sorts. All and nothing. Pre-existence. We can call it the pre-universe. So this being, all alone, uttered the first word ever spoken. According to this book, they said it in the original language; Sanskrit."

"The first word ever spoken by this being was "*aham*". It translates to 'I'. So this was the creation of identity, of separation, of ego. There can't be an I without another." I pointed to the 'I' on the napkin.

"And with this separateness, with this single utterance, the rest of the universe came into being. All the people, all the trees, all the animals, and so on."

She picked up the napkin and looked at the letter. "So the idea is that we are all one I having the thought of separateness?" she asked gently.

"Yes, exactly," I said taking the napkin back and putting it between us on the table. "In a reading, one idea can mean many things, and an image can become symbolically applicable as well as literally meaningful. The image of a man walking with a bag over his shoulder can mean being aimless, or it can mean a new journey. It could mean returning home, or it could simply be an image of a man carrying a bag over his shoulder."

I continued. "The letter 'I' here is the same. We can look at it in multiple ways. We can look at it like a drawing too. This drawing says what an intuitive reader does." I pointed to the top horizontal line of the large capital letter 'I'. "This top horizontal line is the above, the world of the symbol, heaven if you like."

"This bottom horizontal line is the physical, literal world." I pointed to the bottom horizontal line. "The vertical line between the two is the intuitive reader. They are the bridge between heaven and earth– between the world of metaphor and the world of cause and effect." She gripped her necklace and moved it back and forth around her neck as she furrowed her eyebrows.

"Like you're playing with the unconscious mind?" She dipped her finger into her glass and started drawing an 'I' on the table with the alcohol.

"Yeah, you could say that." Her amber brown eyes were hypnotically fixated on the bridge of my nose.

I continued. "It's apart of my job to make the unconscious, conscious; and to integrate the conscious into the unconscious. Not just in our heads, but in the real-world. Symbiotically.

There are two layers to everything, always. The symbolic layer which is also the unconscious, the all is one layer, the God layer, the eternal layer. Then there's the literal layer, the conscious layer, the causal layer, the ego/duality layer."

"The job of the intuitive reader, in my mind, or at least one of the jobs of the intuitive reader is to be the mediator between those two worlds. To be the custodian of symbols, the keeper of dreams. But these two worlds must be symbiotic or things can get dicey."

Modern Ritual

I flipped the napkin over and carried on. "For example, I recently gave a reading to an older man. He was asking what he needed to focus on in this transitional time of his life. I allowed three cards to intuitively come to my mind. At the left was *The Emperor;* an older distinguished man sitting in his throne looking to his right. To the right of *The Emperor* was *The Tower*; which holds the image of a castle burning down violently. To it's right was the third card, *The Fool. The Fool*, a younger man turning his back on the older man and *The Tower*, walking away from the same chaos the king couldn't look away from (*Figure 1*). These images have symbolic representation as well as literal. The literal interpretation was an older distinguished man seeing his kingdom burn down while a younger man turns and walks away from the problem."

"The symbolic understanding of these same images shows that my sitter, an older distinguished man, has two options in a way. He can turn and face his failings, sit calmly, and responsibly accept what has gone wrong. Or he can turn and embrace a more youthful, escapist mentality and continue running. He had a choice to be the king or the fool. To face his problems or to run away."

(Figure 1)
The Emperor, The Tower, and The Fool
Of The Noblet Tarot de Marseille

"You are everyone in your dreams!" she said, tapping her hand on the table with considerable excitement.

"You are everyone in your dreams, yes! And to give a reading is to create a dream which is often more clear and honest than real life. You can choose not to see a situation, but a reading is much more condensed, simple, and direct. You can ignore the nuances and complexities of everyday life. You can't ignore a king watching his castle burn. It needs to exist literally as a simple image, but also symbolically as a representation of this person's actual life."

"What happened with that man though?" she interjected.

"Most of my sitters see me at least once a month. It's a continued process. He came back to sit with me and I gave him another reading. This time the three cards that entered my mind were the same king, looking at the same burning tower–but this time, instead of a young man running from the problem, there was a younger woman looking at the king behind him. The third card was *the Papesse*, not *The Fool* "

"So I could see my sitter chose to address his problems and not run, and now there was a woman interested in him. The only issue was that he was unavailable to her because of his fixation on the problems."*(Figure 2)*

(Figure 2)

The Emperor, The Tower, and The Priestess,
Of The Noblet Tarot de Marseille

She put her palm on the table and leaned in.
"But once someone knows what the problem is, how
can they change? How can they take what happens in
the cards and apply it to life?" she asked with some
fieriness.

"A nice way to integrate the symbolic and
causal is through ritual. Ritual is the human
intersection of unconscious and literal. Ritual is a
performance for the spirit."

"In the process of the reading, there is a kind
of performance. A kind of ritual intended to blend the
unconscious and the conscious into a fluid moment

of clarity. There's a moment of light when the world in the cards and my sitter's world come together. What they need to do is integrated in that moment of realization."

"How does that look?" she asked skeptically.

"People come and see me. They sit in front of me and we just talk openly."

"How often does that even happen?!" she added.

"Our undivided attention is the rarest most valuable thing we can give someone. I give my sitter my undivided attention and I find out what their focus for this reading is. Perhaps it's a question they have. An issue facing them. A decision to make. A relationship which needs addressing. Or anything they feel drawn to talk about."

"Does that usually resolve cleanly?" she asked, darting her eyes around.

"It's ongoing and evolutionary. I try to create some sense of progress though. I use my intuition to give them ideas, to give them a story, images, and answers, if all goes well. This is our modern ritual."

Crashing

I leaned back and finished my beer. "There is what happens to you in your life; the symbol. And then there's what it means. Deciding what it means is the reading. Interpreting the symbol is the reading. It's always different, often beautiful."

"That's a wonderful way to look at the world." she said, leaning in for the first time. "Everything is a means for symbolism. Everything is a door to another way of seeing. I bet if someone were to integrate your intuition with symbols they'd flow through life."

She continued with a soft smile. "Sometimes I feel like the act of living my life; making decisions, talking to people, everything that goes into living–sometimes it just feels like this trudging chore. It's confusing, it's tiring and it feels like I'm swimming upstream. But when I live as if in a dream– when I focus on things flowing, almost by intuition-"

The room was suddenly swallowed by a deep silence. We embraced it and stopped speaking for a moment. The music returned and just as quickly as it came the silence was gone. She continued. "When I'm feeling the natural rhythm of life, everything becomes so much easier, so much more fluid and life becomes a wonderful adventure. I imagine that's what a reading can offer people. It's a way to flow, instead of crash."

They're Just Cards

"So, what are you connecting to when you give someone a reading?" she leaned in further, waiting for a clever answer.

I smiled and said: "I don't know. That's one of the most powerful things a reader can say. I don't know. I try to be honest with whatever I see or whatever comes up, but ultimately you have responsibility for your own life. I'm only here to offer clarity and guidance. I use a few oracles though."

"What's an oracle exactly? Like a crystal ball?" She held her hand out in front of her mimicking the silhouette of a fortune teller gazing into a crystal ball.

"An oracle is like an extension for your intuition. Oracles are like the tarot, numerology, astrology, psychometry."

"Psychometry?"

"It's what I did with your bracelet. These kinds of systems can help open up my intuition, and direct it in clear narrative ways."

I continued. "Oracles also keep me more objective because I read the images that my intuition generates instead of my assumptions. These tools are like a diving board to jump into the swimming pool of intuition. It helps ground the ideas and translate them in the simple universal language of story. That's another beautiful part about using oracles! They allow for visual communication, which is never interpreted the same way twice."

"Oh, you mean like that man with the bag over his shoulder? Or the king and the fool walking towards or away from the burning castle?" she said suddenly.

"Yes! People make the mistake of giving all the credit to the oracle; worshipping the tarot or whatever. But these tools are usually quite innocuous. It's like worshiping the golden calf instead of the spirit itself. "

"The tarot for instance, was not initially created as a tool for readings. The first deck was not passed down by a secret sect of esoteric wise people. Tarot cards were originally just another card game—actually similar to modern-day bridge. Like other card games, the first recorded tarot cards arrived in Europe in the 15th century."

"Like many early playing card decks, the tarot, *tarocchi* in Italian, had suits, trump cards, and pips; now the major and minor arcana. The widely circulated notion of giving intuitive readings with the deck didn't come until the late 1700s when a Frenchman named Jean-Baptise Alliette published the first complete guide to tarot card reading along with a revised deck specifically designed for giving readings. He assigned a specific meaning to each card bringing in ideas from astronomy and the four elements. This would be the first of many interpretations of the cards."

"Wait, what?! She said, hitting her palm on the table top. "So why does everyone have a cow over the magic of the tarot cards?"

"I like to think about the tarot cards like an anthropological snowball. Someone built it, for one reason or another, and slowly, over time, it rolled down the hill collecting meaning. People kept adding their two cents, and more people came along to respond to those responses, and so on."

"Although the imagery itself draws heavily from christian iconography and does hold some anthropological, archetypal, and psychological power, the tarot deck was originally a gambling game and not a sacred energized object as so many believe."

"I don't know how to feel about that," she said with a nervous laugh.

"For some, this may be deflating, but I feel it's inspiring. It's not the object that creates the reading or sees answers to complex personal questions, but human intuition channeled through an otherwise mundane collection of images."

"Do you still trust the many interpretations of the cards at all?" she said, as she began to spin her pen just above the table. "Like how the *Death* card means transformation or *The Fool* means new beginnings?"

"Yeah, I do use historical interpretations of the images. It's important to have a thorough understanding of the traditional meanings, but only in order to completely forget them. The many interpretations can be interesting as long as we're not tethered to them. To be fixed to one definition of an image is to destroy the purpose of the cards as a medium for intuition. Intuition isn't fixed, it's fluid. So to just memorize a bunch of pre-set meanings and relay them is not intuition."

"I almost prefer my sitter not to know any of the traditional meanings associated with the cards. I've done readings where people will see one card come down on the table, whether at random or through my intuitive selection, and they will begin crying. Because to them *Justice* or *Death* is always a bad card, and has a definitive meaning."

"And for them at that moment it does I suppose," she said with a little giggle between her teeth.

"One of the benefits of a reading is to transcend fixed ways of thinking. So to have fixed understandings of the cards cuts off intuition and narrows our journey to a single path."

She scooted her chair in and moved her drink aside, making room for her open notebook. "How do you use the images then? I bet that's hard for some people to grasp. I always felt the cards were charged in some way– that they have some sacred force within them. I've even seen psychics charge the deck with my touch, or with crystals."

"It's much more freeing to consider that the deck of tarot is simply a collection of images. The images are beautiful and leave so much room for interpretation. That openness in and of itself makes the tarot an incredible object. But sacred? Charged? I'm not so sure."

"By leaving the interpretations up to intuition– your own intuition, the images become a stimulation for storytelling. That's a true reading. A reading from *real* intuition, not many other people's recorded intuition."

"It's the difference between going to that real unconscious space and relying on the experiences of others. First-hand intuition v.s. second hand intuition. To read the cards is not to remember what they say, but to actually look at them and read them. As if for the first time. To use the tarot like this– truly intuitively– is to allow the images to reflect without any bias or pretention. The reflection, once we fall into it, becomes a more honest way of understanding a question. The tarot turns the ordinary into pure lyrical honesty. Like a child's view of the world. A mirror which changes what it reflects, to show what it really is."

Shadow, Reflection, Projection

She began feverishly writing in her notebook then suddenly stopped. "So the image becomes more real than the actual experience? It looks back at you unflinching? With you as the reader allowing everything to remain neutral? A guided dream that is more real than a real illusion?" she inquired hastily.

"Well, when we look at an oracle it often serves one of three functions. We can see a shadow, a reflection, or a projection. A shadow shows what isn't there; what we feel is missing or neglected. It can also show the darker half of a situation; the element we have left behind. The aspect that refuses to leave us until it is resolved. Usually, it's the area we don't want to acknowledge. Like my sitter who didn't want to pay attention to his castle burning."

"The reflection shows us what is; what we most want to see, or what we are looking for. It's the reason when someone sees a card they don't see the image for what it is– they see their situation reflected in it. And they begin to fall into the image. It's the reason the figure of the king in *The Emperor* card comes to represent my sitter who's looking at it."

"The projection shows what we haven't seen yet. It shows what we are missing. The projection is the lesson learned when we are able to incorporate the elements of the shadow– what we wish to ignore– with the reflection– what we want to see. The projection happens when the symbolic and the literal worlds collide into a three dimensional experience the sitter can fall into. That falling is the reading."

She closed her notebook and placed her uncapped pen at the edge of the table. "And by the end of the reading, they have a clearer more directed path? Guided by intuition and your neutral eye?"

Slowing down considerably I answered. "Exactly." She leaned back in her chair and it was quiet for a while. The bar hummed on with the soft sounds of strangers chatting by candlelight.

"So how does an intuitive reading look? It seems like the images are not as important as the process of engaging with them."

"Yes! The reading is literally me passing my intuition over these images. Over images that enter my mind. Over words or numbers that enter my mind. It's free form and different every time. It's not about the objects, it's about you and I."

At that very moment, the silence of the room was broken when the bartender realized there was no music playing and hastily played something. *Here, There, and Everywhere* began to play. Our symbolic world had united with our physical one. We were ready to begin the reading.

4

The Anatomy of an Intuitive Reading

With the song from her dream still playing I began. "So what's important about getting a reading today? What are you hoping to get out of our time?" She thought for a moment then began nervously tapping her pen against the granite tabletop.

"I've been working for this company for a few years. I like my work, and I like the company. I'm wondering if it's time to branch out and do my own thing though."

I uncapped my pen and opened to a blank page in my notebook. "Can I borrow a piece of jewelry or something you've had on your body for a little while?" She patted her pockets sheepishly then opened her purse removing a pair of eyeglasses.

"Will these work?"

"Do you have a ring or something that's been on your body?" I said, looking at her fingers.

She put her glasses down on the table and slipped a slim silver ring off her right middle finger. I reached into my pocket and grabbed a black stone. We exchanged the ring for the stone.

I took the ring, still warm from her hand, and placed it in my closed fist against my stomach. Something about holding an object that's been on someone carries something of their memory. If you've ever held something that belonged to a distant relative– you can almost feel a little piece of them in the object. It's the difference between a pen you just purchased and a pen your great-grandfather used every day for twenty years. You can feel them in it.

"Just keep ahold of the stone during this process." I held her ring against my stomach and closed my eyes taking a deep breath. Immediately an image of a racetrack entered my mind. Cars speeding by, looping around a fixed track. The next image was of her and a man ice skating in *Rockefeller Center*. The ice was thin and cracking. There were two small children with them, also skating. I opened my eyes and handed her ring back.

I looked down at my notebook and immediately wrote what I had seen along with three numbers; four, six, and one. I began to see her face as belonging to some of the tarot cards. I got the sense of some colors, postures, and overall energies emanating from her. Next, I matched those details to a few tarot cards from my memory. *The Magician, The Chariot,* and *Temperance. (Figure 3)*

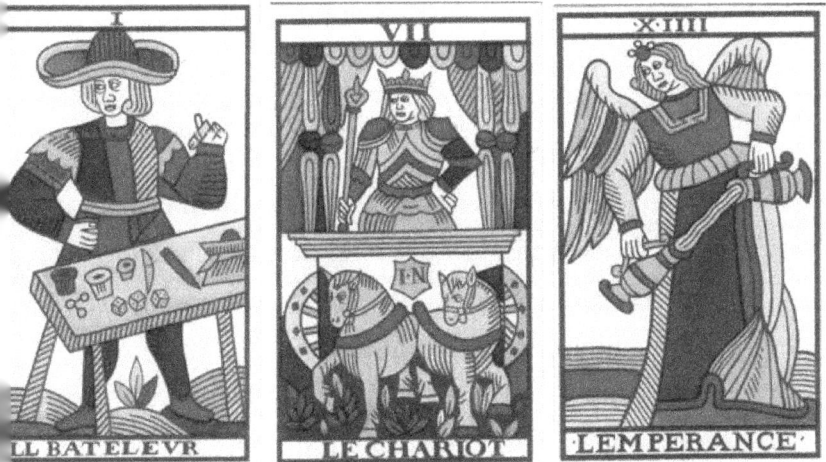

(Figure 3)
The Magician, The Chariot, and Temperance
Of The Noblet Tarot de Marseille

First, the standing scarce posture of *The Magician*. Standing with no fuss, working at a table. Next, the elevated regal posture of *The Chariot*. His armor encrusted with jewels and gold. Finally, the calm and transcendent energy of *Temperance*. I didn't see the images necessarily. I felt the images. I saw them superimposed below my sitter's face.

I looked through the deck and pulled out the three tarot cards without showing her. "I prefer to use my general feeling to select cards for a person, at least in the beginning. Just pulling random cards leaves it up to the cards themselves, as opposed to my connection with you."

"But then couldn't you influence what cards come up? It's not really random" She inquired. I continued shuffling the cards putting them down to answer. "Sometimes just drawing random cards is helpful. I prefer to use random cards when someone is asking a question that requires a binary answer or something about a future outcome. But when it comes to the guidance of something more nuanced, especially during my first reading with someone, I prefer to use my actual intuition."

"There's always intuition involved in interpreting the cards, but to turn over random cards is relying more on fate than intuition. In the beginning, especially when I'm just starting to connect with someone, I prefer to use my natural knowing. I just look at you and allow a few cards to enter my mind based on what I feel. Like I said before, I'll just look at you and tell you what I see and feel. *I'm* giving you the reading, not the cards."

She looked at the face-down cards anticipating the images. "It's important that you take everything I say with a grain of salt though. I'm just looking at you and telling you what I feel, and what I see. Anything that's helpful or clarifying use and benefit from. Anything I say that isn't helpful discard. Use what's helpful, forget what isn't. The goal of this is to be helpful. Also, everything I'm going to say will make more sense to you than to me." I don't intend to, but upon saying this I almost always unconsciously turn my palms up and shrug. It makes me feel like Peter Pan.

She smiled and added. "That's *wonderful*. The goal is to be helpful. I like that." I got the sense as she said this, particularly at the word 'wonderful', that she wanted to stand up and hug me.

I looked over my notes for a moment realizing immediately it was my duty to completely forget about them and focus solely on her. I continued. "So the first idea I saw when holding your ring was a racetrack. Many cars moving quickly around the track. So I get this sense of running yourself in circles. There's definitely a need to keep busy. To keep moving. But lately, you've felt that your moving hasn't been heading anywhere. So I'm certainly seeing that idea of running in circles here. Going nowhere fast."

"The second image I got was of you and a man. Maybe a romantic partner. The two of you were ice skating at *Rockefeller Center.* The ice was very thin and cracking. There's enjoyment here, maybe with someone close to you. But you feel it's going to be short-lived. In the short term you're happy, but in the long-term there's less stability, and you can sense that. Does that make sense?"

She began smiling and laughing a nervous sort of laugh. "Well yes, it does. I definitely have been running in circles lately. Although my day to day work is great– I feel it isn't going anywhere. I feel I'm stuck on the same winding road. I was just telling my husband I feel like I'm on a road to nowhere actually." She paused for a moment nervously laughing again. I consider this kind of laugh mid-reading as a release. When I work with people they release all manner of emotional energies, in a variety of ways. Some yawn, some laugh, some cry, some just sit in silence. There's a lot of processing going on.

She continued, "My Dad passed away in the last year and a half. He worked for a company all his life, and he loved his work, but I could always see he was a little dissatisfied. He wanted to build his own ideas, and he never did. He was enjoying the short-term benefits, but he ultimately never had anything to show for it. I see that same pattern in myself. I just don't know if now is the right time for me to branch out on my own."

I began underlining ideas in my notebook and started again. "There's definitely this sense of a winding road in circles, and moving along but not arriving anywhere. Also, this sense of enjoying where you are now but feeling a little soured by the knowledge it will all fall apart soon enough."

"You know what's also crazy!? My husband and I have been talking about starting our own business together. He's dissatisfied with his job too. It's funny because I work for a production company that does work for *Rockefeller Center* every year during the Christmas tree lighting. So he's probably the other person skating with me in what you saw."

"And funnily enough I was just talking with my husband about our driveway and how it was all iced over. I was joking with him that it was like an ice skating rink. That was literally right before I came to meet you here. You're weird."

"So this is definitely a very real feeling you have about going nowhere fast. You feel the ice beneath you cracking, even though you're enjoying it for now. *The Magician* in the *Marseille* tarot is someone working, he's standing looking quite apathetic, uninterested. He's gazing off to the left."

I turned over the first card and pointed to *The Magician's* stark expression.

"Next to him is *The Chariot*. This card's focus is another individual, now physically at a higher position, up on *The Chariot*." I slid the second card over and pointed to the soldier driving *The Chariot*, positioned above the horses. "He's gained some status and some power; the armor and the scepter he now wields. Being propelled forward by forces under his control; the two horses. There's a sense of moving up but it's still not fully all yours. *The Chariot* is a soldier, representing a larger empire, a growing power. He's a force for someone else's vision. This is probably where you are now. Going from working at something you're not excited about, to working at a higher more powerful level– but still apart of an organization, as opposed to being an organization unto yourself. You've probably moved up within this job and gained more status."

"Yes, that's the thing." she interjected. "Although I've been feeling somewhat dissatisfied with my job, I'm constantly moving up. I have more people working under me, and my pay has gotten a lot better from when I started."

I jumped in, pointing to *The Magician*. "You can see he goes from the humble working of *The Magician;* dressed in simple clothes, doing simple work, two feet firmly planted on the ground; to *The Chariot's* gold and jewels."

I shifted my attention from *The Magician* to *The Chariot*. "There is an increase in power and status. But if you look at both of their facial expressions, there is a constant dissatisfaction. Both are looking off to the left, longingly."

"I actually started in the field. I would be on site, on my feet all day." She pointed to *The Magician* standing, working with his hands. "Now I work more in the office, at a desk" She pointed to the base of *The Chariot* itself, as she mentioned her desk. "And I actually have two people working under me" she said drawing attention to the two horses pulling *The Chariot.*

Die to the Past

"What about that last card?" she said, pointing to the final face-down figure. "Ah yes, this is coming together in an interesting way. The last card is *Temperance*." I turned over the final card and we both looked at the couth angel pouring water from one vase to another. The angel hardly noticed us at all. "Doesn't *Temperance* mean patience and balance? Finding the best way to integrate?" she said, almost nervous about the card's supposed meaning.

"Sure, it can mean that. It's best not to be beholden to the traditional meanings. It's great that you've done some research and know these ideas, but that is only one idea. We have never been sitting here on this night, in this place, at this particular time, in your particular life, with these particular cards. So it doesn't make sense to fix our understanding on the previous thoughts about these cards. We need to look at the cards as if for the first time. We need to practice being simple-minded. Which is much harder than it seems. The only way to give a *real* reading is to give a reading devoid of platitudes and clichés."

She flipped through her notes and circled a few words putting her pen down. "How can it be real if it's all imagined? How can a waking dream be real?"

I looked at the three cards spread on the table and paused looking over their every detail. "In order to be *real*, we must die to the past. We need to let go of the need to hear what we want to hear. We need to let go of the need to hear what comforts us. We need to *be* with what's actually there. That's the only way to be free here."

I considered for a moment. "Giving readings has really taught me that two opposing ideas can be simultaneously true. The images and ideas presented here aren't real. And yet in their shadow, reflection, and projection of your life, they become more real than your own thoughts about your life. You're too close to your own experience to truly see it without prejudice."

"If you look at the progression of the cards from *The Magician* to *The Chariot* and finally *Temperance* you will see the development of power, status, and influence. We see *The Magician* standing, humbly working, dressed in simple cloth, transitioning to *The Chariot*, encrusted in jewels and gold. *The Chariot* is a card of empirical force, a soldier serving a cause, at a higher position."

"The shift from the status wielding servant of *The Chariot* to the singular power of *Temperance* is so clear here. If you look at the angel of *Temperance* you can see she takes up the whole card, she's so calm and independent. She's powerful. She's the primary focus of the card, not just a part of it. She's also pouring the water from vase to vase, fluidly focusing. She's self-directed– independent. Her force and power are staying within her hands, flowing freely in a self-contained way. The angel here isn't exerting herself towards an outward goal like *The Chariot*. The angel is also not dissatisfied and humbly working like *The Magician*. She's maintaining that power for her own aims. The angel is fully in control of herself, and empowered in that freedom."

She leaned closer to *Temperance*, taking in the fluid zen-like movements of the angel's tools. All in stark contrast to the dutiful coldness of the other two cards. She leaned in so close to *Temperance* that it seemed her nose was about to touch it. She pointed to *The Chariot* and *Temperance* with her first and middle fingers. "The angel looks so much more in control. She's less outwardly powerful than *The Chariot*, but she's more self-directed."

I pointed at all three cards with the first and second finger of my right hand, and the first finger of my left hand. "What I see in these cards is professional progress. Starting as an entry-level worker." I pointed to *The Magician* at his table. "Then there's a development of status, but still serving another organization– perhaps with others beneath you. Working with more power but still just being a dutiful servant" I pointed to *The Chariot,* his gems, and gold, his scepter, the horses below his desk like vehicle. "Despite his power, he's a soldier for another."

"There's this development of serving yourself– maintaining your energy for your own endeavors. You're keeping that focus within your own intentions and directions. And you can see there's an increase in personal power. You're reaching your highest self as a literal angel" I pointed at the hands of *Temperance,* easily and peacefully swaying the energy of the water, keeping the center of gravity within herself. I continued. "The angel in the image also takes up much more of the card than the previous two figures. This indicates a shift in focus from the job itself to your personal identity. Finally, there's the look of calm on her face. She's at peace."

"So ultimately there's a progression of power. You're going from working for someone else's vision to a reclaiming your internal focus towards your own aims. You're definitely starting your own projects or businesses. Doing so will allow you to be your highest self. There is a loss of some physical status, and income at first." I pointed at the shift from the gold armor of *The Chariot* to the humble robe of the angel in *Temperance.* "But you'll be much more fulfilled, and in control. You'll also be the focus of your own time and energy."

The waiter dropped by, gently placing a small white candle at the center of the table. The room began glowing a hue of midnight sunshine.

She looked at the three cards and their progression from left to right. It's like reading a triptych in a gothic church. "Hmm, so I guess I'm starting my own business! I'm excited, I should go call my husband and tell him about this. I know he'll be happy. He's been telling me the same thing. It just feels so good to see it here in a visual way, all laid out. And I understand what you were saying before about seeing what *is,* rather than what we want to see. I can see the progression in the cards; it's unmistakable. You can't think your way out of it or argue with it. It's right there staring you in the face."

I broke eye contact with the candle to chime in. "Well, it's not only about the cards. One of the distinctions of an intuitive reader is that the reading is based on my sense of you as a person. What my intuition tells me about you when I look at you. With a psychic reading, it's all about the cards, or the tea leaves, or the palm, not the person as a whole. A psychic reading is about telling a future, not exploring a life. I use my intuition channeled through the oracles, to express what I feel from *you.*"

"I *love* that!" she sang. "It's you and I using the oracles as tools instead of the other way around."

Something Else

As I looked at the cards I began to notice something odd in the pattern. "These cards show a progression towards your goal. But you seem preoccupied with something else. It feels like there's something else weighing on you. This isn't the full story. The reading is saying you'll get what you want but there's a malaise over your eyes. There's something else here we're not talking about." I looked down at the three cards, seeing the progression, but feeling something was missing. I noticed all three figures' eyes."

"They're all looking off to the left towards the same spot," I said pointing to each of their three sets of eyes, and then to the spot at the side of the table to the left. Their attention was fixed to the same point.

I continued. "All three figures in all three cards are doing their work, their respective tasks. But all three are looking off to the left. It's as if they have something else on their mind. All three are looking towards the exact same spot. There's a progression of independence and power among the cards, but there's something more. Something's happening under the surface. There's a collective longing. You can see it in where the attention is."

"It's like when you're talking to a friend, and they're zoning out, or not making eye contact with you. They seem preoccupied. You're making progress in your career but you're not present for it. There's something else missing. Something more important to you isn't being fulfilled."

"You are getting what you want, but you're still not fully satisfied here. There's something else taking your attention away. There's something else you are still focused on. What's this over here?" I said, pointing to the spot on the table, the three figures were fixated on. "Until you address that missing piece you'll never be satisfied."

She stared fixated on the one point to the left of the cards. "I don't know. But I know what you mean. I thought I would be more excited by the prospect of starting my own business and having that control. It does feel like there's something missing, and all this talk of career is almost beside the point. I am excited to start my own projects and to be more in control, but I don't feel fully present. What is that?" she said, pointing to the same spot on the cold smooth table.

Altered States

"Would you like to find out?" I closed my notebook and capped my pen, sliding both to the far corner of the table. "Would you like to find out what that distraction is? What is keeping you from being present in this transition?"

She looked over the cards, and back to that spot on the table, before looking up towards me. "Yes, I think I need to know what that thing is. Otherwise I'll quit my job and start my own projects, but still feel dissatisfied. Like that thing is missing." She continued looking over the three cards and their singular gaze.

"Generally at the end of a reading, I do some trancework with my sitters. I do it to cement the ideas we talked about, or to gain more clarification about what the reading brought up. This would be a perfect use. Do you meditate at all?"

"Yeah, I meditate, every now and then. It helps me relax my mind after a long day."

"The trancework I do with people is very similar to meditation. We're interested in using these altered states to integrate the ideas that come up during a reading. The trancework can take us the rest of the way towards discovering what we need to know. It can access our own inner oracles. The trancework can help us understand what we need to do. It helps us integrate."

"Is it like hypnosis?"

"Yes exactly! I use generative hypnosis. Which is trance, but not with the intention of fixing a problem or a bad habit. We're using hypnosis here to explore the deepest parts of ourselves, and to integrate new more positive ways of being. The reading guides, while the trance integrates. It brings the ideas from the reading into our first-hand experience. I find the two modalities compliment each other very well. It creates a more complete process."

"Yes, that's amazing. I'd love to try it. I've never heard of someone using hypnosis during a reading."

"Okay great!" I said, slipping my jacket off onto the back of my chair. "So first off, get yourself comfortable. Put your feet flat on the floor. Rest your hands in your lap. Take a deep breath in, and hold it for a moment. Now exhale and feel yourself sinking into your chair. Now I'd like you to fix your gaze on the flame of that candle."

She took a deep breath and immediately began slipping into a wonderfully comfortable space. The dancing candle flame drew her in, and immediately her eyes had a comfortable shimmer over them.

"Trance is essentially a space of intense relaxation and intense focus. It feels quite familiar and comfortable. If you've ever had that moment right before you drift off to sleep. That moment where you are aware of your environment. You can still hear things. You're conscious, but you can feel yourself drifting to sleep, and the next thing you know you're waking up. That's trance. That space right in between being awake and being asleep –that's trance. And as I speak with you now, only really aware of the sound of my voice, you can begin to feel yourself relaxing with those big deep breaths."

"You can feel yourself rooted into your chair quite comfortably drifting away, with your eyes still open. And if it's even more comfortable you can close your eyes now. But at some point soon, looking at that flame will begin to make your eyes feel quite tired, and at that point, you can just close your eyes."

"As you sink and float and drift all the way down to a wonderful trance-like sleep, my voice will be right there in the center of your mind and floating all the way around you. My voice lifting you up into a wonderfully calm, warm dream state, here in this space."

"The amazing thing about a trance is that every word I say and every breath you take can allow you to sink even further down into this space. As you sink down, you are drifting into the deepest part of yourself. The part where your unconscious mind lives. Your unconscious mind has all of your potentials. All of the wisdom you'll ever need– it's only a matter of access."

By this point, her eyes were closed and her head drooped down into her chest. There was a slight smile inching its way across her face. In my experience people in trance access a level of peace and clarity they rarely experience. All this happens at speeds which rival the time it takes to check your email.

"Now as you feel yourself really sinking down into this space– feeling the light of the candle dance across your face, we are going into the deepest parts of your unconscious knowing. Deep breaths, sinking deeper and deeper down now. In a moment we're going to talk with these three tarot cards. This is, in a way, an imagination game. But as we know from dreaming, imagination can offer so much more than we could have ever imagined. Or as much as imagining can imagine about imagination."

Imagination Game

"So we've been looking at these three cards for quite a while. We've been seeing their facial expressions. We've been seeing their energies. You have the images of these cards locked in your mind very well– even unconsciously. In your mind, approach the first card, *The Magician*. Nod your head when you see him in front of you." There was a short pause followed by a small nod.

"Good, now I want you to ask him what he's distracted by. What is that thing he's looking at? Off to the left. When you ask him you will almost immediately, without any hesitation, be given an image. It's important that you trust the image and don't second guess yourself. It's going to feel like that answer is only imagined, and it is. You are, in a way, channeling what the card has to tell you. Just allow one image to enter your mind. What is he looking at?" There was a look of concerted effort on her face.

"You don't need to *try* to do this. It will just be done. You can ask him and you will see a visual answer. Nod your head when you've done that." There was a much longer pause this time. I could see the strain in her face again.

"Ideally this is done very lightly, no effort exerted. Just the first thing to pop into your mind's eye. There's no wrong answer, only the one you see." She immediately took a deep breath and sank deeper into her chair, and in doing so, sank deeper into the trance. "Perfect, now let me know when you've seen a response from *The Magician*. Literally just imagine him showing you what he's looking at. Nod your head when you see what he's showing you. Like in a dream."

There was a long moment of searching. Her head slowly nodded. "What is he showing you? You can speak and remain in trance?" I asked, leaning in to hear what she would say.

In almost a whisper she said what she had been shown. "I saw a big house. But it was standing empty. It felt cold" I leaned away jotting down what she had seen.

"Okay, you can shake that image away and go even deeper into this space of trance. That's wonderful, you have a very powerful imagination." There was a brief moment of restriction, then she sunk even deeper into her chair, letting go of the first image.

"Great, now we're going to talk with that second card; *The Chariot*. This card was an increase in power for you. We want to know what he sees in that same spot, off to the left. Take another deep breath, hold it for a moment. I'm going to touch you on the shoulder, and when I do you can sink ten times deeper and more relaxed. Letting that breath out, sinking inside of yourself. Really melting into the air around you now." I moved in and touched her shoulder. "Exhale now and let it all go." She let out the breath and reached a profoundly deep space. Her eyes were flickering as if in a REM state of sleep.

I Want to Build Something

"Now we're going to draw our attention to *The Chariot*. Just as with *The Magician* before we are going to ask the charioteer what he sees off to the left. You will receive a visual answer. That card and its knowledge have integrated into you from this time working with it. These images will create images in you. Now ask him what he sees. Ask him what is distracting him to the left. What is keeping his attention split? What is pulling him away, despite his power and status?"

"Just as before, you will see an answer. There are no wrong answers. Nod your head to let me know when you've been delivered a response. What is he looking at over there?"

She nodded her head and immediately began speaking in a low hushed tone. "I'm seeing that same large cold empty house. Now it's on fire though. It's slowly burning to the ground. It's ember." She grimaced and I immediately intervened.

"That's okay, you can view the image safely and comfortably far away– seeing it objectively. And just as easily as it arrived you can allow it to fade away. Like the end of a movie when the screen fades to black. Let it fall off of you." I touched her shoulder and swayed her back and forth. The tension of the image left her body.

"That's very good. Your imagination is incredibly powerful. And as is often the case, your imagination can address issues with a wisdom we don't have access to in our waking lives. Continue sinking down now."

I jotted down her second image to the right of the first. I was beginning to make a three-card tarot spread from her imagination. A triptych of her deepest thoughts. A visual language to give us insight into what she was being distracted by. Something was weighing on her so heavily she was unable to consciously address it. We had the first two of three images. A house, and house burning down.

"Now we'll slowly shift our attention to the angel in *Temperance*. Ask her what she's looking at off to the left. She'll show you. Ask her and wait a moment." This time she immediately nodded her head and began describing the image that came to her.

"I see myself. But I'm older. I see myself older. I'm playing with kids on the floor of a living room." I touched her shoulder again swaying her in this trance space. "That's great. This image came to you even more quickly than before. Let that image go. Feel it drain out of your body through the bottoms of your feet."

She relaxed the tension in her shoulders and sunk even further down into the chair. The candle was beginning to burn low and flicker in exhaustion.

Our empty drinks sat drying. We were among the last people left at the bar.

"Now it's up to you to look and see for yourself. Look and see what that thing off to the left is. That thing pulling you away. That thing that's been distracting you. You can turn your head and look to see it. An image or an idea, something will present itself to you. The culmination of our time here. Much like we've been doing with seeking the help of the tarot cards. Now you can look and see it without any help. Whenever you're ready."

She nodded her head and sat breathing very deeply. Deep breaths into her belly. Her chest was extending and contracting. Finally, she turned her head to the left to look at what she needed to see. She remained there for a moment before turning her head back towards me. She immediately began breathing quickly. Her eyes popped open and she began crying. A small smile crawled its way across her face and laughter followed. I handed her a napkin.

"What just happened? Talk me through it." She padded the napkin against her eyes and laughed again.

"Well, I saw myself with kids and a home. I saw myself building something, but not just a business or a career, but a family. I don't have any kids. That's something that has always been at the back of my mind. As I've been focused on my career I felt I was running out of time."

"Running out of time to do what?"

"To start my own family. I guess I want to build something other than my own business."

She continued laughing, smiling and crying. "It's interesting because it seems you started working for this other company wanting to build a family, a home. The three images the cards showed you demonstrated that. *The Magician* which represented the start of your working career was looking to a house, but it was empty. Then *The Chariot*, representing the growth within that work, was looking to that same house, but on fire. That sense of home, or the striving for a home, was slowly being destroyed.

Finally, the angel of *Temperance*, which showed you becoming more professionally independent, was looking at you playing with children in that previously empty house. It's not just independence in your work, but in your life. It's not building something in your work, it's building something in your life. Then you saw what was keeping you from enjoying your work."

She nodded her head and brought her attention back to the three cards. They rested above my notes of the images revealed to her. "Yes, that's exactly it. I want to build my own home, my own family. And I really feel like this is something that has been weighing on me. Something that has kept me up nights. My husband has been talking to me about it recently too. He wants to have kids. I was just afraid it would become my entire life, or that I wouldn't be able to work. But if I build my own business I can work from home. I can be in charge of my own life. That will allow me to build a whole life now too, not just another job. Thank you so much for this. Can I take a photo of these cards?"

"You can keep them," I said, pushing the cards towards her.

"Are you sure? Don't you need them?" she said, gently brushing them apart. I looked down at *Temperance* with her swaying vessels. "No, they're just cards."

5

The Trail is Beautiful, Be Still

"The idea is to remain in a state of constant departure while always arriving. It saves on introductions and goodbyes."
-Richard Linklater

Something about Chelsea seems friendlier. Walking from midtown Manhattan towards West 20th street I see people growling, spitting, moving coldly forward. But as soon as I get to 21st and 9th ave I see mothers with strollers, waving at neighbors in the crosswalk. Everyone seems to be smiling. I get the distinct sense that no one below 24th street spends Thanksgiving alone.

I turned the corner at West 8th and ducked into a small cafe. Fortuitously snagging a seat by the window I sat facing the door awaiting my friend. I have the habit of arriving ten minutes early and preparing in my notebook for meetings–although I never use what I've prepared.

He arrived dressed in all black carrying a long umbrella. He said hello to a few other patrons and finally the owner behind the counter before sitting down with me. I ordered a coffee and a madeleine. He got a beer and French fries.

"So good to see you," he said moving the silverware to the far left side of the white granite table. "How are you?" His fingers interlaced and were joined by a quick smile.

"I've been pretty good. I haven't been remembering my dreams these last few days."

He shrugged. "When I can't remember my dreams I remember that I can walk home in a dream, and see the birds in a dream, every day. Why reserve your dreaming for the sleeping hours?"

"Like a daydream?"

"Well, sort of. It's like what Joseph Campbell said."

"Follow your bliss?" I hesitantly added.

"He did say that, but he also said "A dream is a private myth, and a myth is a public dream.""

"A dream is a private myth."

"Yes, and a myth is a public dream." he chipperly added.

"The Tarot is a collection of public dreams."

"Yes, used to create private myths."

"The tarot cards are universal and everlasting because they encapsulate the human experience and the human responses to those experiences."

"They're primordial," he said in a sing-songy way.

"Yes. The intuitive reader makes the timeless malleable and timely. It is the reader's job to apply the images, meanings, and energies of the Tarot, the collective myth, to the sitter. This makes the larger story relevant to the individual's myth." I somehow always slipped into speaking in rhythmic patterns with him.

"When I think of the individual's myth I think of the individual's story. Their story surrounding their job, their marriage, themselves, their mental health." He looked behind me at other patrons eavesdropping on us.

"Well, there's the collective story– what we know as a culture– what's normal. Then there's the personal story. The dynamic which really causes a lot of pain is what the individual wants and needs v.s. what the larger culture offers."

"How do we find our place in something which operates without us?" He pointed his first finger in the air reminiscent of the painting of the death of Socrates.

A Flexible Bridge

"How do we find our place in a world which operates without us? The answer to that question is always changing for an individual. And how they answer defines who they are, and how they get along in the world. The intuitive reader is the bridge between cultural myth and personal dream. The reader helps weave a story for the sitter using intuition, and a deep understanding of the rich symbols of the tarot."

"But isn't being too dependant on the tarot dangerous?" he said, playing devil's advocate.

"Do you think so?" I countered.

"Yes, I do. Worshiping the symbols is equivalent to taking religious stories literally. When the mythic story loses its ability to adapt, it becomes a prison. People become trapped by the imagery of the tarot."

"That's the difference between a psychic reader and an intuitive reader. Flexibility, and fluidity. The emphasis is on personal development and growth– not quick easy answers to abate the existential woe that comes with being a face in a sea of faces." I darted my eyes out the window and saw a woman sitting on a red bench with three very large dogs. She was waiting for someone. Perhaps another dog.

"Ideally a relationship with an intuitive reader is evolutionary. It's always moving with the life of the sitter. With a skilled intuitive reader, someone may find a compelling story, and come to better understand their connection to the larger culture they occupy." He took his hat off and placed it on the table in front of him.

"The reader is like a weaver of beautiful, relevant, clarifying stories using the powerful language of personal myth." I saw him follow each word with a movement of his eyes and a small smile. Like the bouncing ball of a sing-along.

A True Reading in the Face of a Stone

Our drinks arrived. I dropped a sugar cube into my coffee and began stirring with a tiny wooden spoon. "Oh man, look at this. There are the four suits. Clubs, Hearts, Spades, Diamonds. Right there on the side of the coffee mug." I pointed to four splotches of coffee on the side of the cup– which looked exactly like the four suits of a deck of cards.

"You should take a picture of that," he said taking a sip of Belgian beer.

"Yeah, I will right now." Taking my phone out to take a picture, I continued. "I've been noticing patterns in the bark of trees and turning the images into readings." I snapped a photo and looked at the results.

"Yes exactly. Like tea leaves, or the patterns of clouds in the sky. See! You can enjoy your dreaming during the day. Any time you can find stories in shapes you are dreaming." he said, gently plucking a few French fries.

"I was just reading about this Lakota Sioux shamanic practice called *rock-seeing*. The shaman would think about a problem they'd like to have an answer to and wander out into the wilderness looking for a rock large enough to fit in both hands. They would wander until they were drawn to a specific rock. A rock they were pulled towards, through some outside force"

"When they found the right rock, the shaman would pick it up and carry it to a quiet place where they could sit with it. The medicine person would then look at one side of the rock and begin to ask the question. They would stare at the rock and wait until figures and images appeared in the natural texture of the stone. They would then repeat this process three more times on the other three sides of the large rock. The shaman would then take all the images and figures from the four sides of the rock and weave them together to develop a reading– an answer to the question posed."

"That's a true reading. A reading before the tarot, or any other imaginary solutions. Using the clouds, rocks, sand, and water. Interpreting the patterns of the world," he said pulling out a black fountain pen.

"What's interesting is that the shaman believed the *rock* was giving *them* their answer. They didn't believe they were using the rock to get the answer. They believed that the singular universe was speaking to them through a piece of it. It wasn't about them. It was about the connection to something infinitely bigger than them– but at the same time, a part of them."

"I've heard of shamans taking sitters into the woods to find a stone for themselves. The sitter would find the stone and interpret the images on their own. The shaman being more experienced would naturally help them with additional interpretations. It was a facilitated process of finding answers in patterns." I dipped my madeleine into the coffee and began stirring with the pastry.

Who's Asking?

I pulled my chair in and lifted my coffee to take a drink. The coffee left a stain on the napkin in the shape of an octagon. Like a watercolor painting.

"That's actually what I wanted to ask you about today!" He pointed emphatically towards the stain on the napkin. An eight-sided shape is just an eight, which is two circles. Like this."

He slid over another napkin and began drawing two intersecting circles like a Venn diagram. "You have separate elements. You have the patterns in the rock. You have the three tarot cards on the table, or the images that come to you when you hold someone's object. You have these separate elements–just images."

He pointed to the two circles of the eight. "As soon as these ideas come up during a reading you are looking for the intersection– the point of union in them, to create an answer, or a story to address the person. You are taking these separate entities and marrying them. As soon as they intersect you create something new– something that wasn't there before. And at that intersection, we have an answer. At that intersection, we have contact with something we are apart of– something much greater than us." He drew a little star at the intersection of the two circles. "The middle of this metaphysical Venn diagram. The union of these intuited, seemingly unrelated images, creates the reading."

I picked up the napkin and examined the two circles with the star at the intersection. "That's how the image of a house burning down, and a woman playing with kids on the floor can mean wanting to have kids."

"Yes exactly! And what those images mean depends on the question, and who's asking."

"I find so many people just want to hear their ideal outcome. They come in having an expectation. They already know what they'd like me to say. But I can't play that game. My job isn't to make people feel good about what they already know. My job is to be the one out of tune key on the piano."

"What about people who are afraid you'll tell them something they don't want to know? About their future for instance?" he asked.

"A lot of palm readers and psychics will tell people definitive things. They talk about soul mates– destiny. They talk about what will, or won't happen. All of that limits choice. All of that restricts people's notions for their futures. I'm not in the business of limiting choice. I'm here to give people more options, not less. I want to give them perspective, guidance, and clarity on their lives. I don't want to tell them what will happen, and what won't happen. That's limiting. That's damaging."

"When people go to see the average reader they are sacrificing some of their freedom in exchange for a hollow sense of validation or security. The path is long and we have to choose for ourselves. I want to give my sitters more strategies. I want to give people more perspective on the path I want to help guide them towards a beautiful future– not a false, comforting one."

"I know. But how can you argue with what people want?" he asked, once again playing devil's advocate.

"It's okay if people don't want to work with me. It's a commitment, and it's work. Most of my sitters see me at least once a month. Our work together is ongoing. But at least I can warn people because the world of readers is really slimy."

"Absolutely. Half my week is picking up the pieces of a harmful reading someone got in the past." he added.

"People get taken advantage of. They get flattered, and told comforting things, and sent on their way. I want to be fair and honest when I work with people. I want to really add value to their lives. Even if people don't want to work with me, I want them to be careful who they do work with. There's a lot of ill-intentioned readers out there."

There was a brief silence in mourning for all the misguided readings that had been done.

He rotated his frosty beer and continued the thread of our conversation. "I had this friend who saw a reader. She was told that her ex-boyfriend was her soulmate and that she needed to fight for the relationship– no matter what. The only problem was, her ex-boyfriend was in another long-term relationship. He had moved on. But this reader gave my friend a false narrative. A damaging story. Because it's what she thought my friend wanted to hear. It was toxic and restrictive. My friend became obsessed."

I stirred my coffee washing away the marks of the four suits. "I want the insights ultimately to come from the sitter, not from me. Which is counter to the notion of the intuitive reader being the source of wisdom. Real change, real insight, needs to come from within the sitter. My role is to spark the fire and stoke the flames. The real work happens within them. If they become dependant on anyone's advice, that's not growth. That's not real change– that's dependance. I've had some consistent sitters that I've seen every week for years. But I'm never doing the work for them. I'm helping guide them through their work."

"I know what you mean." he interjected. "One of the major things tarot has taught me is that life moves in cycles. If you push when you need to be pulling– you suffer. If you pull when you need to be pushing– you suffer. If you rest when you need to be moving– you suffer. If you move when you need to be resting– you suffer."

"It's like there's a natural harmony to everyone's life. A reading illustrates strategies to move through the cycles of life gracefully. Intuition allows us to know whether we need to be resting or moving– pushing or pulling."

The door to the cafe opened and a group of about six people piled into the small restaurant. It suddenly became too loud to speak quietly. The rush of people passed by and the stillness of the place came back.

"Ebb and flow." I continued. "I see an intuitive reading as a check-in. It's there to ensure that we are moving through life gracefully– harmoniously. I think everyone has had the experience of being in harmony with their own life. Things flow easily. We are effortlessly joyful. Quicker to laugh. Quicker to smile. We feel full of life."

"That's when life is a dream. And likewise, when we are out of harmony, just being awake feels like a struggle. Things don't go our way. We feel as if we have bad luck. There's friction with the world." He finished his beer and rested for a moment.

"A reading is to see where we are with the natural rhythm of our life, and to get back on track," I added.

"But it doesn't feel like work does it?" he said, pulling out the major arcana from the *Dodal Marseille* tarot deck, one of the very first tarot decks in print.

"No, not at all. Intuition is basically using your imagination towards problem-solving. Towards seeking. It's imagination put to work. It can reach so much more, and be so much more than analytical thought alone."

"How do you mean?" he asked, mixing the cards.

"Well, for example, if you are struggling with an issue or a question, you can close your eyes. You can imagine yourself in the future after you've already solved this problem. You can ask your future self how they solved that problem as if it were already past. You will hear an answer from your future self. An answer from your future self who already solved the problem. This future version of yourself will tell you how they figured it out."

"Is that image of your future self your imagination? Or are we time traveling in a way?" he asked.

"I have no idea. But either way, people get solutions to their problems. Solutions they couldn't have thought of otherwise. My sitters who try this claim they are being told solutions from someone else."

"Like looking to the tarot deck for answers?"

"Yes, but that's only one small part of an intuitive reading. It does help."

"To ask questions of a stack of cards is ridiculous. That's exactly why you can get an accurate answer." He placed the deck face-down on the table.

I spilled a little coffee on the table just shy of the cards. I moped it up with the napkin still baring the octagon drawing. "Just like asking a question of your future self is absurd. But that's why it works so well," I said.

"It allows us to transcend the traditional ways of thinking. Which have within them many traps."

"Yes, and they are giant rusty bear traps. If someone gets stuck in them it can be quite painful and difficult to break."

"And that's the beauty of using intuition. It doesn't try to break those traps– it just dissolves them. If we fight against the traps of thinking– the treadmills of life– we struggle harder and their grip on us gets stronger."

"But to address life with intuition, with imagination, and with the visual imagery of the tarot is to dissolve the traps, to dream them away, or to realize they don't exist at all."

"They never existed. We are the one trapped. We are the traps themselves." he said, adjusting the cards on the table meditatively. "Intuition is about supposing that we already have the answers. It's about supposing that in the act of asking– the answer already exists"

"I worked with this woman over email once. She had lost her ring. She wanted me to help her find it with a reading. So I drew three cards. The first was *The Star*, the second was *The Chariot,* and the last was *The Papesse* or *The Priestess."* (Figure 4)

(Figure 4)
The Star, The Priestess, and The Chariot
Of The Noblet Tarot de Marseille

"In *The Chariot*, I saw the ring as the wheel of the chariot itself. It was under the box-shaped wooden chariot. So it could be under something rectangular– perhaps a piece of furniture. The wheel was underneath the wooden chariot. *The Papesse* was holding a book. So maybe near or under a book. *The Star* depicts a woman kneeling down. So the final reading was: under something large and rectangular, behind a book, low to the ground– you'd need to kneel to get it. I tell her these clues, and within twenty minutes she responded to me saying she found her ring under her bed behind a book. She said she had to kneel down, like the figure in *The Star*."

Who Can Explain These Things

"We have no idea really. And it's all a wonderful game of imagination" He began mixing the tarot deck, gently placing it on the table between us.

"The origins of the tarot for divination relate to a game in Europe from the 1500's. It was a game called *"tarocchi appropriati,"* where people would make poems about the sitter's personality based on randomly drawn cards."

He turned the top card over. *"The Fool."*

"If the fool were to persist in his folly he would become wise," I added pointing to *The Fool's* journey ahead. *(Figure 5)*

He turned over another card and placed it next to *The Fool.* "*Death*. When a sign persists it becomes an omen. When an omen is ignored it becomes a curse."

(Figure 5)
The Fool and Death
Of The Dodal Tarot de Marseille

"Joy impregnates, sorrow brings forth." I pointed to *Death's* scythe. "This is very much the story of the reader." I continued. "We have the beginning of a journey." I pointed at *The Fool* starting his journey. "Then there's a sweeping away– a clearing out, and it comes to an end. First the walking stick of *The Fool*. Starting his journey– feeling his way through. Then the scythe of *Death* sweeping away. With *Death* himself standing up to begin another journey. The reader sees things clearly and sweeps away what is superfluous."

He looked over the cards for a moment then pointed to *The Fool's* upper margin where the *Roman numeral* could be found– but it was blank. "*The Fool* has no number." He then pointed to the lower margin of *Death* where the name of the card could be found– but it was also blank. "*Death* has no name."

He finally pointed to *The Fool's* ambitious stride. "Let's take a walk!" he said, jumping to his feet putting some cash on the table.

How Well We Jump Over The Fire

It was a beautiful day– though a little warm. We started walking towards 10th Ave. Slowly walking we were carefully looking for any clues strewn about. We looked for any symbols to interpret and turn into a reading.

"This is how shamans would give a reading. They would walk into the world looking for omens and signs."

"What's the difference between a reader and a shaman?" I asked, stepping over a generous portion of dog poop.

"Historically, culturally, there's no distinction between a shaman and a reader."

"Wouldn't the shaman use their reading as the diagnosis to an ailment and follow it by healing the affliction?"

"Yes, the reading was only the first half of the process. It was to inform them of the healing that needed to happen. Usually in an altered state."

"So a global, 21st-century shaman would do the same?"

"What do you think?"

"I think the format would be dressed up a little differently– but overall the healing process would be more about getting to a place of psychological and spiritual balance."

"How do you do that with your sitters then?" he asked teasingly.

We stopped at a crosswalk next to an elderly lady using a walker. The traffic subsided and we crossed towards the Highline as I continued.

"I see the reading as directing the course of the work we do. It guides the conversation. Then I use trancework to explore and make changes to the deepest part of my sitter."

"That's what shamans do."

"The logical next step after a reading is to address what was brought to the surface."

"We also serve as great transparents." he said.

"Great transparents?"

We climbed the stairs of the Highline and began walking towards the Whitney Museum.

"Yes, André Breton– the surrealist– had this idea of the *Great Transparents*. They are these figures who come to us in times of great crises, dressed in all black. They come with keys to unlock the situation."

"That sounds like a shaman as well."

"Yes, but it's more– transparent. I've come to think of a reading like that. But instead of offering the key, we offer the lock itself. The sitter already has the key. The answer is found in the act of opening the lock. The answer is found only once the right question is asked."

"It's not about what we see in a reading– it's about what it means."

Suddenly there was an explosion of car honking down on the street. Someone had tried to turn right but was blocked by pedestrians. Cars behind him were holding down on their horns. Someone was even sticking his head out the window yelling at the turning car to "come on!"

"I can always tell my mental state by how I behave in traffic. If nothing can bother me in traffic I know I'm in a state of peace." he said, nodding.

"For me, it's brushing my teeth. If I can brush my teeth without feeling any sense of impatience or annoyance I know I'm in a great mental space."

He stopped and looked up towards the sky. There was a small gap between two skyscrapers—exposing the bright blue sky and a small fluffy cloud nestled between them. He sat on a bench looking at the perfectly framed entity.

"See that cloud there?" he said, pointing up.

"Yes, I do," I said, sitting down next to him. We sat for a moment watching the little white fluffy cloud. It was gently visiting Chelsea. A plane passed over the cloud mimicking the arrow of *the Lovers* passing through a delicate heart in the sky.

"Just keep looking at the cloud there. Keep watching it." he said.

The cloud sat motionless for a moment then began to lightly vibrate. The edges condensed and the cloud began moving very subtly to the left. The changes were so delicate I thought it was just my eyes adjusting at first.

"Keep watching," he said as he looked on.

The cloud began to get lighter. It slowly shrank until it was a thread of itself. He lifted his hand up towards the cloud and mimed rubbing it out– like clearing a chalkboard. In that final gesture, the cloud had disappeared. He looked on for a moment at the perfectly clear blue sky.

"Aristotle said that tragedy is a mixture of terror and pity. But wonder is a mixture of terror and joy. So the difference between tragedy and wonder is the difference between pity and joy."

He paused for a moment taking off his black jacket. He continued. "Life will always be terrifying– confusing, complex. The difference between a life of wonder, and a life of tragedy, is facing that terror– not with pity for our lives, or ourselves– but with joy at the absurdity of having existed at all." He slowly stood up turning to me. "Enlightenment is to be surprised at everything. It's to always feel tickled. To live as if in a dream."

I Had Time

We walked down the Highline past fussy kids and young couples. I could see the Whitney Museum peeking out over the horizon.

"I think they have some Duchamp paintings. They came from Italy before this."

"He's the guy who put the urinal in the museum right?" I inquired.

"Yes, among other things."

"I love that. Art is context. If you fix a car in a garage you're a mechanic. If you fix a car in a museum you're an artist."

"Context is important. But so is confusion."

"I'm confused."

"Confusion is a blessed state, as Milton Erickson would say."

"It reminds me of my first visit to Europe."

"Tell me about it."

"It's like you were talking about before. Terror and joy."

"It was super humid and cold. Fresh rain sunk into my well-worn converse. I stumbled down the northern Italian cobblestone streets. Next to the city center, I waited for my bus back to my then girlfriend's house."

"It already sounds like a painting." he added.

"The last number four bus was to come at 1am, and it was 1:15am. At that moment another number four bus pulled up on the other side of the street. I ran across the street and hopped on. As the bus pulled away I saw across the street, where I had been waiting, a number four bus arriving. It was the one I had been waiting for but abandoned. I immediately knew I made a mistake."

"Our bus pulled off carrying only a few tired travelers. We passed house after house and went onto the highway. With every mile we drove I felt more lost– more terrified, and confused. I asked the driver if we were heading in the right direction. Not speaking Italian I told him the address I was heading to. He pointed behind us with his thumb. We got off the highway and the number of passengers slowly whittled down, until it was just me, the driver, and another older man."

"We got to the end of the line. It was an industrial and mostly empty area of the city. We arrived at a fenced-in parking lot filled with buses. Across the street was an open field consumed with weeds and stray cats. I turned to look at the other passenger; an older man dressed in a Hawaiian shirt and shorts. He looked horribly out of place. He stared directly into my eyes. He said with a cosmic calm and a seamless American accent 'You have time'. Was he a spirit, a hallucination, or some surrealistic figment of my imagination?"

"Or all three!?" my friend interjected.

"One of my great mentors later told me that "*God*" speaks to us through strangers. Every now and then, in trying moments, I hear that old man's voice telling me that I have time. It helps."

"The bus stopped and the driver nudged me out. I stood there on the empty sidewalk as the bus pulled into the parking lot and the gates screeched closed. As the sound of the closing gates escaped the immediate air around me, a dead silence sunk into my bones. A moment later the driver walked out of the gate looking plump and jolly, holding a lunchbox. He walked me over to a nearby bus stop. He stood there with me until another bus pulled up, from what felt like thin air."

"I was confused. Extremely confused. We both boarded the ghostly bus. My guide sat down and started joking with the other driver. After a short drive, my guide and I got off the bus. He pointed down a long street– smiling. I pointed in sympathy with his outstretched arm, non-verbally asking if it was the right direction home. He smiled and nodded.

I hugged him and took off. The columns lining the sidewalk rushed by in blurs with the raised stones cast in orange light beneath my feet. I could read the graffiti on the five-hundred- year-old walls as I passed. I ran, and ran, and ran, never seeing another person."

"That sounds confusing. I'm glad you made it home. I think perhaps, I've met that same old man on my trip to Toronto." my friend innocently said. We were about a block away from the museum when we passed a homeless man leaning up against a brick wall. He shouted at us as we approached. "Pay attention!" he said. On the brick wall behind him was a small graffiti sentence written in black ink "The trail is beautiful, be still."

We both looked at each other knowing our time together was over.

"When we are ready the sign will appear." my friend said– turning to thank the homeless man and handing him a folded bill. He turned back to me and said: "I'll see you soon!" He turned around and walked towards the museum entrance.

"Definitely! Enjoy the museum!" I said waving and swiveling around. I walked down the stairs of the Highline towards my sitter's building. I had to get to West 10th in ten minutes, but I had time.

6

Zap, Apprehension, Career, Hell

"The aim of life is to live, and to live means to be aware,
joyously, drunkenly, serenely, divinely aware."
                              -Henry Miller

I arrived at my sitter's building a couple minutes early. On the glass door to the lobby was an etching of a griffin in gold. On either side of the door were two off-white pillars. The image was immediately reminiscent of *the empress* or *The Priestess.* I could tell this reading would be about bringing in some feminine energy– or at least balancing the masculine.

I buzzed him and the door swiftly opened. The building was entirely made of brick on the outside and had a gold hue on the inside. I arrived at the twenty-third floor and the elevator doors opened. He was outside the elevator waiting for me.

"You're right on time!"

He ushered me into his apartment. We sat at a table by the window and he poured me a cup of coffee.

"Oh, thank you."

"I'm pretty much always drinking coffee."

I pulled out my notebook and immediately wrote "feminine energy."

"Already having some ideas?"

"Yeah, I write whatever occurs to me, as we go. So I don't forget."

"Are you just writing your first sense?" he asked, as he sat holding a large white mug of coffee.

"I find my unconscious mind knows things before my conscious mind is able to catch up."

"Oh yeah? Is that like some Freudian stuff?" he asked, adjusting his glasses.

"Well not exactly. Our conscious minds do a lot for us and are quite intelligent, but our unconscious minds are a hell of a lot smarter. All of our fears, dreams, latent potential and subliminal knowing lives in the unconscious."

"So you're saying it's better to work unconsciously?"

"First there needs to be a deep level of study and mastery. But once you've devoted yourself to something it becomes apart of you. Your unconscious mind can pick up on so much more and digest it exponentially quicker."

"I have to be honest with you, I'm highly skeptical about intuition and psychics and all that stuff. I'm an atheist– I believe in science."

"Giving a reading or relying on the unconscious mind is not an act of belief, but an act of agnosticism. You can't be absolutely sure of anything. That makes one open to anything. Which is what's required to really use your unconscious mind."

"Is that absolutely the case?"

"Maybe," I said through a tight-lipped smile. I took a sip of my coffee and hit record on my phone. "Is this okay for you?"

"Of course! Can you send it to me when we're finished?"

"Absolutely. I like to record all my sessions so people can listen back later. Perhaps you'll keep discovering more from our time here. What it means will always change."

"Oh like a painting? I was at the Whitney today, actually."

"Oh yeah? I just came from there. And exactly like a painting. If you go and look at a painting it could bring up thoughts, memories, feelings. If you were to go back to that same painting a year later you'd find a whole new experience."

"I think it's the same with any art."

"Yeah, exactly. A reading is like a piece of art made just for you. Made for this particular time of your life. Do you have honey by any chance?"

"For your coffee?"

"Yes, honey softens it up."

"Yeah sure." He went into the kitchen just behind the table and continued speaking. "So you don't take what you say so seriously huh?" He opened an overstuffed cupboard looking around for the honey.

"Like you're not into telling people heavy shit about their future?" He came back with the honey and a spoon. "Here you go. Honey and coffee, I'll have to try that." He sat down silently awaiting my answer.

"What's more important than what I say is what it brings up in my sitters, and how it directs us towards being more clear or making some change. It's the inciter of change."

"So what you say isn't the end of the work? It's the beginning?"

"Yes."

"I'm a consultant and that's basically what we do. People think we're there to do everything for them but we're just there to help them do it for themselves. So where does what you say come from?"

"Like I said, I'm agnostic. I just come in, take a deep breath, go into a light trance and close my eyes. What I see and feel is what pops into my mind. It's based on an understanding of the tarot and other things– but a lot of it comes to me like how you'd see something in a dream."

"And you said it was unconscious, correct?

"It has to be. Which is why when there's pressure, or when I force it, nothing really happens."

"That makes sense."

"Yeah, it's like PWA. Have you heard of perception without awareness?"

"No, tell me about it."

"Well, PWA is one scientific explanation for psychic abilities. We are exposed to so much information in our surroundings, at such a continuous level, that our brains have to edit out what seems less important– and only see what's more crucial."

"Oh yeah, I've heard about that."

"It makes sense when you think about it. By entering into a trance, or by accessing your intuition, you aren't just accessing your conscious knowing– which is the stuff that your brain actively hangs onto. You are accessing your unconscious knowing– which is the stuff that you're in touch with but not really aware of. The stuff we aren't aware that we're aware of is most everything."

"That's a lot."

I finished my coffee and moved it over to one side of the table.

"It's only a lot if you get in touch with it consciously. Because you can't know what you aren't aware of knowing. You know?"

"I think."

"It's more feeling than knowing. At least at the unconscious level. There was this famous American hypnotherapist, named Milton Erickson who would enter a light trance before all his sessions. He did this in order to access his unconscious knowing."

"It sounds like his sitters were the hypnotists."

"Ideally, we enter into the practice of healing together. It's a mutual agreement to make-believe– together."

"Make-believe what?"

"I always say that my job as a hypnotist and as a reader is not to hypnotize people, but to help them shed away the trance of the world. I'm taking people out of a trance. I'm helping people make their own beliefs."

"I can get behind that. I've never gotten a reading before, but my good friend, someone I trust the opinion of very much, said you could help me. I'm not usually into this kind of stuff but it seems your approach is more psychological. It seems you work to guide and help people. I just hate the idea of someone telling me what will or won't be, you know?"

He continued, "I'm in the world of finance. So when someone tells me they know what will happen tomorrow, or in a year, I know they're bullshitting me. I spend all day, every day, around people claiming to know what will happen in the world– and none of them know for sure. No one knows. Do you know?"

I laughed and shook my head. "I'm not into that either. I want to help people be freer– be more whole. I want to help people be happier. These are the tools I use. I find so much of the process of healing lacks something absolutely fundamental."

"What?"

"Magic."

"Now you've lost me again." he said, pouring me another coffee from a steel carafe.

"Thank you. Well, I don't mean like *magic*, magic. I mean that sense of possibility– story telling. A huge part of healing, real healing, is the sense that anything can be created– anything can be changed."

"Can it?"

"Absolutely. Especially when you enter the world of the unconscious. The world of symbol. The world of dream."

"Why do you think that is?"

"If you address a problem at the surface, you'll get surface results, and surface change. But if you go into the unconscious, if you go into the dreaming of a person you can make a deep lasting change. All because it's unconscious. Playing is a big part of unconscious work. So it's fun."

"I like fun."

"Most do! Some people can feel heavy about our work, but the moment I am commenting on picture cards, and putting them in a deep trance, things lighten up. Things float."

"Picture cards? You mean the tarot?"

"Yes, they're just pictures for us to make new dreams. Pictures for us to channel our experience through. And when we change the picture, we change our experience."

"Like changing the picture in our heads?"

"Exactly like that! Or like the Lascaux cave paintings."

"How do you mean?"

"Well, you know about the Lascaux cave paintings?"

"Yes, from the Paleolithic era? The cave paintings that are about twenty thousand years old?"

"Yes exactly!"

"What about them?"

"That's a good example of a reading," I said adding more honey to my coffee and stirring slowly. "These ancient peoples made simple paintings of animals with spears in them. They did this so their image would mimic their reality and they'd have a good hunt. It was early sympathetic magic."

"We're back to magic, huh?"

"It's not magic in a fairy godmother way. It's magic, in that it's human beings changing their internal world, to change their external world. Inner control to gain outer control. When we look at the cards we are seeing our situation in those cards, and so we gain perspective by shrinking everything down."

"Can we change the cards to change the reality?"

"We can change the cards to get a sense of strategy, and then use trance to bring in your unconscious mind's innate ability."

"So our unconscious mind is the magic?"

"The magic is all that is possible. Our unconscious mind has all our capability lying in wait."

"Like buried treasure?"

"The analogy I always share is that your unconscious mind is like a genie's lamp. It can give you anything you ask for. You only need to ask– and be specific."

Pieces of a Story

He got up and went into the kitchen for a while. He came back holding a small floral plate covered in chocolate rugelach.

"I love these things." he said, eating a whole one before he set the plate on the table between us.

"I grew up eating these. So, what are you hoping to get out of our time together?" I asked, grabbing a chocolate morsel.

He finished chewing his rugelach before taking a big swig of coffee.

"Like I said I'm pretty skeptical about this stuff. I have to say, you've really opened my eyes to all the layers of this kind of work."

"I'm glad," I said, dipping my rugelach into my coffee.

"I want you to tell me what you see– or what you feel from me before I go into what I want to address. Is that okay?"

"Yes of course. That's a more traditional way to see a reader. They give you a sign without any information at all."

"So no answering questions?"

"We value answers more than messages now. It wasn't always that way. People used to travel for miles to get a sign from a healer. The idea was that we have the answers already living in us. What we don't know is what we aren't even aware of. That's where the message of the reader comes in. It's showing us where to focus our attention."

"Great, show me."

"Can I borrow an object that's been on your person for a little while? A ring, necklace, something like that."

"Will this work?" He pulled off a heavy black ring with a regal crest.

"Yes, that'll work. It's still warm."

I took the ring in my closed hand and put it next to my stomach, closing my eyes.

Immediately I felt the warmth of sunlight and saw clear blue Caribbean water. Then came the image of a casino. Those images and feelings passed and were replaced with the image of a white stone fountain, in a cemetery. Next, came four words. Zap, after, career, hell. Next, the image of *The Emperor* entered my mind. Followed by *the wheel of fortune*. I quickly jotted everything down. *(Figure 6)*

"Looks like you got a lot there." he said, peeking over my hand.

"Sort of. It's pieces of a story we fit together for you."

"Tell me."

"The first images that came to mind were of a Caribbean island. Crystal clear blue water. A casino. The next thing I saw was a white stone fountain in a cemetery. Almost stucco."

"Oh wow, that's pretty good Lucas."

"How do you connect with that?"

"My family has a house and some land on a French Caribbean island. There's a little town nearby. In that town, there's a cemetery. In that cemetery, there's a white stucco fountain. The island has a casino, and the water is definitely crystal clear blue," he said with a Cheshire grin reaching across his face. "I've been wanting to go back actually. It's been years."

"That connects with some other ideas that came through as well. There's a shift in career. Probably moving from a hellish situation into something less so. There's a zap of energy after escaping a hellish work situation. That zap of energy is a little overwhelming and you're not quite sure how to direct it. But you're in control and comfortable. I'd say that change is reverberating through the rest of your life too. This is definitely a time of self-fulfillment."

"Wow. I have to tell you, that's really spot on. I'd say you were talking to someone about me." He let out a hardy but nervous laugh. "I just quit my job because my boss was a complete putz. So yes, a lot of change, but all my choice. Now I'm kind of at a loss. I don't know what to do with myself. I have a lot of energy to work with though. It's like I've been struck by lightning since I quit my job."

(Figure 6)
The Emperor, and The Wheel of Fortune
Of The Noblet Tarot de Marseille

"The first card that I had for you was *The Emperor*. He's the king. He's in control– comfortable. There's this masculine powerful energy. He's the means of grounded universal energy. He's all about manifesting that energy into the physical world. You can even see him with his lightning rod." I pointed to *The Emperor's* scepter and then back to the word "zap" I had written.

"I'm the king? I like the sound of that." He moved his mug over and turned *The Emperor* around to look at it more clearly.

"Yes, there's a lot of viral energy here. Masculine energy. The ability to create and yield power over yourself and others. But there's an apprehension about using it. Maybe you're afraid of this energy –or you don't know how to use it yet. Does that make sense?"

"Yes, it does. I've always had this ability to assert power, or just get things done in that fiery way. But I often feel I lose control of myself. I feel it's too self-serving– too aggressive. I don't want to do harm by asserting what I want."

"The king doesn't just assert what he wants, he grounds energy and builds a kingdom. Building a kingdom not only benefits the king, it benefits others. A family, a group of people. That energy can be used to serve others." I pointed at the crest on the shield by the king's side. "He has this crest here. This is his kingdom. His people, but also his creed– what he fights for. The Emperor's not only serving himself, he's serving an ideal."

He paused for a moment then responded. "That Carribean island you first saw; it was hit really hard by last season's hurricanes. People were devastated. I've been thinking about going and doing some work to help out."

"Yes, that would be a great use of masculine energy. The zap of energy the king is capturing is being channeled into grounded usefulness." I pointed to his scepter in his one hand, and his other hand on his belt.

"You see he's grabbing his belt with the other hand– grounding the energy. It becomes more stable, and sustainable by grounding it into real-world service."

"I've been needing to get a new belt for a while now!" He grabbed ahold of his belt and pulled it above his shirt to show the tattered leather.

"I would definitely get a new belt. Something that The Emperor inside of you would approve of. Ground yourself with it."
"I will."

"Using your energy in service of others is a wonderful way to become comfortable with your masculine power. By using it to benefit others you are gaining control over the energy."

He pulled his chair in and leaned back looking up towards the ceiling; presumably thinking.
"Anything else I should know?" he said playfully.

"Yeah, there's a couple more things."

Called to Something

He began staring off over my shoulder. I turned around to see what he was looking at. There was a large drawing hung on the wall behind me.

"I like that drawing," I said admiring its simplicity. *(Figure 7)*

(Figure 7)

"Oh yeah. Sorry, I was just zoning out."

"Where did you get it?"

"I found it actually. Well, it was sort of given to me."

"Sounds like a good story."

"Not a very long one. I found it sitting out on garbage day, by the curb. It was just sitting there, frame and all, in a pile of garbage. I'm not the type to take things out of the garbage. Far as I'm concerned, something in the garbage is garbage, and I ain't touching it. But I was just walking down the street, on my way to work as a matter of fact, and I was arrested by an image. Stopped in my tracks by half of this image sticking out a pile of garbage bags. I stopped, and immediately pulled it out of the garbage to look at it."

"You heard its call?"

"It's what?"

"Sometimes people are called to something. Pulled towards it. Usually, it's an object or a location of deep importance to that particular person's soul. It's important to their growth, or who knows what. You could be on the train, walking through the park, or down the street, and be compelled, magnetically attracted to a moment. Attracted to a discovery of some great totem. For the people who listen at those moments, there's a great unconscious treasure waiting for them."

He jumped in. "A friend of mine hunts for magic mushrooms. He said the trick to finding mushrooms is after you find the first one, eat it, and you will be drawn to more. Almost pulled towards them."

"I imagine it's a very similar feeling. It's like in that moment of being pulled towards that place or object, we are looking back at a memory. As if that moment had already happened, and we were being guided by the shadow of the future memory."

"What about Moses finding the burning bush?"

"Yeah, this idea definitely appears in mythology. Being pulled towards a moment, or an icon of sorts."

"I studied art history in school if you can believe it, and iconography always blew me away. How a motif or symbol can persist in multiple cultures, throughout time."

"What does this icon mean?" I pointed to the drawing behind me.

"I have no idea. That's what drew me to it. I felt I had seen it before, but I knew I hadn't. It was clear and yet confusing."

"There's this Japanese phrase which cannot be translated into English. The phrase is *mono no aware*. In English, it roughly means the awareness of a moment passing. Walking down the street, you became aware of that moment passing, and something inside of that moment, the drawing, pulled you towards it. Being drawn like that, to a symbol, is the world giving you a reading– showing you the path forward. I have some more icons here for you," I said pointing to my full notebook.

"Yes, please. I bet our time is almost up."

"We have some time. But the other card I drew for you was *The Wheel of Fortune*." I pulled out the card and placed it to the right of *The Emperor*.

"So what do these two cards mean, together?"

"We can see the shift here. In the first card, the only figure is the king on his throne. Whereas in the second card we have a smaller man at the top of this wheel, holding a sword, wearing a crown. Below the smaller man, and also on the wheel are two other figures. So the first shift we can see is a king here with his crown becomes a smaller man with his crown. There will be a loss of power once the throne becomes the wheel. Even if you look at the footing of the two figures. The king is rooted in his chair sitting on solid ground, and here the small man is at the top of a spinning wheel. The whole structure is on top of the water."

"So a loss of power?"

"And the loss of stability. But only for the time being. The king must uproot himself to do some kingdom cleaning."

"What about these other figures below?" he asked, pointing to the second card.

"This shift in your use of power and action will involve and directly affect other people. The king's scepter becomes the mini king's sword. Showing off the power you have in the form of a scepter, becomes acting with that power in the sword. The sword is a tool of power in action– rather than the ceremonial representation of power, in the scepter. Now's the time to use your power in action. But things are shifting." I pointed to the mini king's sword and then to the wheel turning.

"I'd say this shifting is a shifting in your power. Maybe you're doing something that is a bit out of your realm of expertise. It'll be uncomfortable, but ultimately rewarding."

"A king becomes a miniature king. A scepter becomes a sword. A throne becomes a wheel. The ground becomes water. Your inner strength and ability are changing."

"I'd definitely say I'm in a reflective time now." He pointed towards *The Emperor's* seated contemplative position. "And I do need to ground this energy. I also need to adapt it to a new set of projects, skills, and ambitions. It's uncomfortable. I feel like I'm starting over in a lot of ways. But what helps is remembering that what I've learned won't go to waste. I just need a new way to channel it."

"Now is the time to stop considering and to take action." I pointed at *The Emperor* sitting and then over to the smaller king on top of the wheel holding the sword. "Things seem calm now because they are. Pretty soon a lot will be demanded of you, and a lot will be happening. Ground yourself now and take stock of that masculine power you have. Think about what your creed is." I pointed at the shield next to *The Emperor* containing his crest.

"The animal in the crest, on the shield, next to *The Emperor* representing your purpose and creed, comes to life in action here on the wheel." I pointed to the animal on the wheel as a living animal in contrast to the frozen image on *The Emperor's* shield.

"I think I need to go back to St. Martin to help fix some of the damage. I haven't been back there in years. That could be a good use of my energy–towards helping others."

"And you need a new belt," I said pointing to his belt. "Remember, it's not just about channeling that energy well, it's about holding it in a stable, grounded way."

"I think I know what that drawing behind you means now." He pointed to *The Emperor's* scepter. Then to the smaller king's sword in *the wheel of fortune*. Then he pointed to the drawing hung on the wall behind me.

"Tell me." I turned in my chair to look at the drawing.

"That vertical line is the scepter, and also the sword. It's also me and my power. The wavy lines are the masculine productive energy coming down into me. I am drawing on this motivation to do good by others. I want to bring it into the world in a solid way."

"And you were pulled towards this image. You were being given this same reading all those months ago. If a symbol persists, it becomes a sign. Before I go we need to get you in touch with *The Emperor*. It's so you can confirm with him, and be guided towards serving yourself, and serving in general."

"Okay, let's do it. How the hell do we talk to a card?"

"We're not talking to the card. The card represents something in you. It's the masculine protective energy, which has made you successful. It's the masculine energy which has manifested your world as it is– but now we need to re-calibrate its efforts. You need to talk to what the card represents in you."

Like in a Dream

"Have you ever been falling asleep, and just before you drift off, you have a little idea, or you almost hear a little voice? It's your voice, but it's very quiet. And that little voice subtly tells you something so true you wonder how you could have ever forgotten. Has that ever happened to you?"

"Yeah, I guess so. When I was deciding where to go to school and what to major in. I remember I was right in the middle of that decision, and one night, just as I was falling asleep, the complete image entered my mind. I saw myself at one particular school, studying one particular major, and I looked really happy. I felt like I was seeing the future. I would say I was just seeing what I wanted to see, but I was seeing it as if in a dream. It's like when you are just passively watching something happen in your mind. It was like watching a movie."

"Yes, like in a dream. It doesn't feel like you are creating the image. It's creating itself right in front of you." I interjected. "That's exactly what we're about to do. Using a light trance. That experience you had was a light trance, and you were accessing some deep unconscious knowing. In this case, we'll be getting in touch with the part of yourself that has all those abilities, and all that energy."

"Let's do it."

"We can begin slowly. To start, you can put your feet flat on the floor, and your hands on your lap."

"Okay." He sat up in his chair and adjusted his posture.

"Good. Now close your eyes, as if you were about to meditate. Take a deep breath. Go back to a time you felt very harmonious– peaceful. It can be a simple memory, a vacation, sitting in the park– it can be anything. A memory from any time. As long as you can picture it clearly. Usually, it's just a moment from a memory. Something that brings up good feelings."

He nodded his head and immediately began smiling.

"That's good. Begin to see everything you were seeing in that memory. Hear everything you were hearing. Feel everything you were feeling. Really go into the space of that memory."

I continued. "As you do this you, can become aware of any tension in any part of your body. As soon as you notice it you can begin to let it all go. Let the chair take all of it. If you notice any tension, anywhere, just let it go. Now I want you to see a door in front of you. On the other side of that door will be The Emperor. On the other side of that door will be your masculine energy. In the shape and form of *The Emperor* we were just looking at."

He nodded his head again. He looked apprehensive.

"It's okay, it's only a part of you. It's a powerful part of you, and it's here to help you. Now the door will open. I want you to nod your head to let me know when you see The Emperor sitting in front of you."

There was a long pause. He took a deep breath then nodded his head.

"The king's friendly, he's here to help you. I want you to ask him how he's here to serve you. When he answers, you can repeat back what he said. It'll be like that half-dream you had. It will reveal itself to you, through the king."

He nodded again and adjusted himself in his chair. I turned around to look at the drawing behind me. It's dancing lines created a comfortable uneasiness. The silence was broken by him softly relaying The Emperor's message.

"The king is saying he's helping me by directing me and by giving me the energy to act."

"Okay, and how does he feel you should act with this energy now?"

"He's saying he's tired."

"We only become drained by success if it is for no greater purpose than our own well being."

"The king is saying he knows what we have to do. He's saying he doesn't have the energy right now."

"Ask the king if the king can channel the energy from someplace outside himself."

"Okay, I'll ask." There was another long silence, again broken by a soft answer. "The king thinks he can. He's saying I need to take the first step towards a new purpose– which will energize him and get him started. The king will carry me the rest of the way."

"Ask the king what you can get started for him." I quickly added.

"It looks like the king is putting down his scepter. The king is saying I need to rest for at least a day." He opened his eyes and immediately started laughing. "My girlfriend was telling me I need to take at least one day off. I haven't had a single day off in three years."

"Go back and talk to the king. Ask him what you need to do after the day of rest."

"Okay, how?"

"Close your eyes again, and relax down. Begin to see the king in front of you. He'll be sitting on his throne waiting for you."

He closed his eyes and quickly sunk down into his chair.

"Once you see the king in front of you, ask him what you should do after your day of rest."

"Okay, he's saying I need to go to St. Martin and help. He's saying I need to stop stalling with Margaret. Oh wow."

He opened his eyes and started shaking his head.

"Who's Margaret?" I inquired.

"That's my girlfriend. My high-school sweetheart. I've been feeling like I'm just stalling her. I don't know what I'm waiting for. We've been living together for four years now. I want to marry her, but there's something in me that's resistant."

"Ask the king why."

He closed his eyes and quickly returned to this trance state.

"Ask the king why you haven't asked Margaret to marry you."

"The king's saying it's because of him." He shook his head and opened his eyes. "What does that mean?"

"Ask the king," I said grabbing the last rugelach.

He closed his eyes and drifted down further than before.

"The king's face just turned into my Dad's face." he whispered softly.

"The king is the representative of masculine energy. Our fathers are our early representations of masculine energy as well. How does your dad connect to marriage though?" I asked, looking down towards *The Emperor* card resting between us.

"My parents got divorced when I was thirteen. Ever since then marriage seemed so stupid. Almost naive. My Dad was very stern about it, but my mom was softer. She was hurt much more than my dad by them splitting up."

"You don't want your masculine energy to hurt Margaret. What else is the king saying?"

"He's saying to take some time to rest, to do nothing. Then I need to go help on St. Martins. He's saying I need to go with Margaret. He's saying to bring Margaret with me and to marry her. He's saying to not be afraid."

He suddenly stopped and there was a long silence in the room. He continued. "The king is telling me to ask Margaret to marry me on the island."

He opened his eyes with a look of fear and wonder. "What the hell just happened?"

"You met *The Emperor*."

"I have to make some calls." He stood up from the table emphatically.

"I think that's a good stopping point for today" I stood up adding. He walked me to the door thanking me again.

7

The Rocks That Grow Again

"God gives the nuts,
but he does not crack them."
-Franz Kafka

The elevator dinged with each of the twenty-three floors as I sunk through my sitter's apartment building. I walked past the two pillars and the gold griffin on the front door.

An ambulance rushed by immediately followed by two large black dogs on the sidewalk. The world was rushing back in. A reading exists in a world apart. Spending two hours with someone in that world and then leaving, creates some altitude sickness.

I hurried to the Port Authority station and made it just in time to catch the eight o'clock bus home. I had a whole row to myself, and it was one of the newer buses. I sat leaning my head against the window, watching the trees cut through the clouds in the sky as the sun went down.

I was thinking about the day and the tarot. The bus hummed on in the darkness. The rumbling lulled me to sleep. I drifted and sank. Just as I was falling asleep I had one of those half awake, half asleep moments. I had a waking dream about the rocks that grow again.

Have you seen the rocks that grow? They sit by the black water on the full moon. It's an optical illusion. I dreamt there was a storm out over the waves. It felt primordial like it wanted to eat me. I wanted to get a better look so I walked into the ocean with my boots on and sea water rushed between my souls and toes.

I walked down the sand and saw an older man with salt and pepper hair dressed as a cowboy. He was holding a prayer candle. The glow lit up the cracks in his face. They looked like the Grand Canyon. He was walking in circles. It seemed like he was looking for something.

I walked up to him and asked what he was looking for. He looked up at me and held my gaze for a minute. He looked confused. Then he said, "I'm not looking for anything."

At that moment I realized that I was looking for something. I was looking for my jacket. I looked down and realized I was now holding my jacket.

The cowboy looked at me as if I had my face on backward. Like he was looking through me. He said something to me, in a voice which sounded like sand and salt.

He said: 'Everything's a metaphor. Life is either a Rorschach test or rattlesnake venom. Live in harmony or in pain.'

He then slowly turned around and walked off down the beach. I could see the glow of the candle slowly drowned by the distance. All that was left was the sound of the ocean crashing against the rocks that grow. Have you seen the rocks that grow?

Special Thanks

Mom and Dad

Enrique Enriquez

Brad Barton

Peter Blum

Kumi Yamashita & Erik Maahs

Elizabeth Levy

Robbie Tharp

All my sitters who I've had the privilege to work with.
Thank you!

Selected Bibliography

Bandler, Richard. *Reframing: Neuro-Linguistic Programming?® and the Transformation of Meaning / by Richard Bandler and John Grinder ; Edited by Steve Andreas and Connirae Andreas.* 1982.

Bandler, Richard, et al. *Using Your Brain--for a Change.* Real People Press, 1998.

Keynes, Geoffrey. *The Marriage of Heaven and Hell, William Blake.* Oxford University Press, 1975.

Campbell, Joseph. *Myths, Dreams, and Religion: Eleven Visions of Connection.* MJF Books, 2000.

Campbell, Joseph. *The Hero with a Thousand Faces.* Yogi Impressions, 2017.

Davis, Wade. *One River: Two Generations of Scientific Adventurers in the Amazon Rain Forest.* Simon & Schuster, 1997.

Decker, Ronald, et al. *A Wicked Pack of Cards: the Origins of the Occult Tarot.* Duckworth, 2002.

Elman, Dave. *Explorations in Hypnosis.* Nash Pub., 1970.

Enriquez, Enrique. *Tarology: Yl, Wy El /WaI /l: Voyelle.* Eyecorner Press, 2011.

Erickson, Milton Hylaud., and Sidney Rosen. *My Voice Will Go with You: the Teaching Tales of Milton H. Erickson, M.D.* Norton & Company, 1991.

Farber, Philip H. *Brain Magick: Exercises in Meta-Magick and Invocation*. Llewellyn Publications, 2011.

Harner, Michael. *The Way of the Shaman*. Harper & Row, 1993.

Mehl-Madrona, Lewis. *Coyote Medicine: Lessons from Native American Healing*. Simon & Schuster, 1998.

"Online Etymology Dictionary." *Index*, www.etymonline.com/.

Pollack, Rachel. *Seventy-Eight Degrees of Wisdom: a Book of Tarot*. Thorsons, 1997.